OLD SURREY RECEIPTS

Mother Ludlam's Cauldron — 3.00 ft. wide.

Gathered by

Daphne Grimm

Published by

PHILLIMORE

for

SURREY LOCAL HISTORY COUNCIL

1991

Published by
PHILLIMORE & CO. LTD.
Shopwyke Hall,
Chichester, Sussex, England

for
SURREY LOCAL HISTORY COUNCIL
Guildford, Surrey

as extra volume number four of
Surrey History

Cover Illustration: **BAKING THE BREAD** from a water-colour painting by Helen Allingham, executed in the 1880s, when she was living at Sandhills, Witley. It shows the housewife removing the bread from the oven with a peel. Note how the mantle ruffle has been caught up out of the way. The oven is placed behind the chimney-stack: a wood fire burns on the hearth and a pot crane is just visible behind it.
(Courtesy of The Leger Galleries, 13 Old Bond Street, London)

FOREWORD

These receipts are believed to have been used in Surrey and range in date from the middle ages to the beginning of this century, with one exception - the Guildford Royal Plum Cake, a pleasing custom which continues to this day.

They have come from a number of books and manuscripts, many in private hands, and have been generously lent by their owners, and it is a pleasure to record their names at the end of this booklet. The utensils that are illustrated likewise come from private collections and they were photographed by Kenneth Gravett, whom I also thank for his unfailing support and encouragement.

As written records these receipts necessarily deal with the food of the literate classes - in the middle ages, the great households; from the sixteenth century, the gentry and by the eighteenth century, the prosperous middle classes. Little is known of the food of the poor before the nineteenth century.

In the medieval kitchen the fire was kept in day and night, all the year round and the men (cooking was rarely women's work in that period) ate and lived and slept there as well. It was often a separate building to reduce the fire risk. The unglazed windows, with shutters only, meant that the cook had to add to his skills the ability to assess the strength and direction of the wind and to adjust the draught (or damp down the fire) as required. Food was stored on racks hung from the walls and ceiling, clear of the rats and mice. Meat was often salted and dried or smoked as was fish, although this could come fresh from the stew-ponds. (In some areas and periods geese, living on water, were considered to be fish and hence allowed when the Church forbade the eating of meat !) A table or dressing shelf, forerunner of our dresser, the spit before the fire, turned by a boy, and pots suspended over the fire, completed the equipment.

The Tudor period saw the appearance of a few books to aid the mistress, allowing her into the kitchen to give orders. Various offices, for example, bakery, dairy and a still room came to be added and the advent of the brick chimney meant that the fire could be contained within a basket, with a back to reflect the heat and a pot crane added. As sugar became available (a refinery was operating in London in the 1550's) the range of preserves widened and a greater variety of foods including fruits and vegetables, initially regarded with some suspicion, expanded the menu for the rich. This continued throughout the seventeenth century, necessitating new markets like Covent Garden, designed by Inigo Jones. The turkeys and tomatoes ("love-apples") were supplemented by pineapples, believed to have been first grown at Dorney Court, near Windsor in 1665, and the new drinks, tea, coffee and chocolate, spread new social habits. Pepys records drinking chocolate at home on 26th. February, 1644 and coffee houses appeared in London some six months later.

In the Georgian kitchen, the open fire in a larger basket could boast a smoke jack and moveable parts forming pot shelves. Windows were glazed and the room lighter. Water was often pumped, but rarely safe to drink, beer being the general drink. Food was frequently of doubtful quality and nearly all records include receipts for 'curing' rust, mould, ticks, etc. By the early nineteenth century, the enclosed fire or range appeared in large houses. In this, heat was

3

THE KITCHEN OF A WEALTHY FARMHOUSE OF THE EIGHTEENTH CENTURY, drawn by Sidney R. Jones for the extra issue of *The Studio*, on *English Country Cottages*, published in 1906. It shows the cooking-pot and pot-crane, the spit-machine mounted above the lintel on the right and the spits, stored with the guns in a rack, also above the lintel. Note also the mantel ruffle, which was believed to help cure a smoky chimney, and the rail for a large overall curtain, so that a settle could be put in front of the fire and enclosed to avoid draughts.

controlled by dampers, widening the cook's scope considerably. By mid-century the middle classes were installing them and also cookery books for the ordinary housewife, rather than the chef, were on sale. Due to the enclosed stove, these writers could give a guide to temperature and cooking times. Probably the best known is that of Mrs. Beeton (1836-65), brought up in Epsom, with many of her receipts perhaps following those of Eliza Acton (1799-1859) (and possibly owing something to the books by Hanna Glass (1747) and Mrs. Randell (1809)).

Mrs. Beeton set out her receipts in the modern form, with the quantities listed first and then the method, and grouped them by subject in the order in which the meal was likely to have been eaten at dinner. In this booklet, I have followed this system, where possible arranging the receipts alphabetically within each course, retaining the original phrasing and spelling.

Perhaps modern cooks may enjoy trying the receipts used by our forebears, while historians may like to consider what was available at the time.

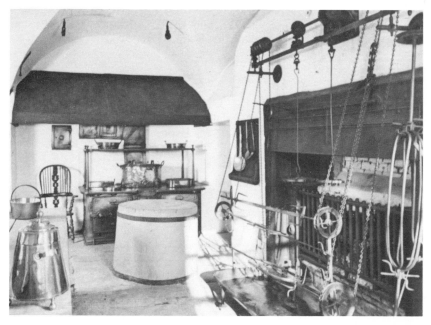

THE KITCHEN AT CLANDON PARK showing, on the right, the fire set up for roasting with the spits placed horizontally in front, with a pan underneath to catch the fat. There is a fan in the chimney, turned by the rising hot air, and this drives the spits through a system of gears and pulleys. Spare spits of different sizes are stood on the right. There is also provision for suspending the roasting meat vertically if the cook so decides.

To the left of the fireplace stands a butchers block and behind this is a cast-iron range, with a separate flue, providing ovens and hotplates.

(Courtesy of the National Trust)

5

SOUPS, BROTHS & POTTAGE

Rules to be observ'd in making Soops or Broths

FIRST take great Care the Pots, or Sauce-pans, and Covers be very clean and free from all Grease and Sand, and that they be well tinned, for fear of giving the Broths or Soops any brassy Taste. If you have time to stew as softly as you can, it will both have a finer Flavour, and the Meat will be the tenderer. But then observe, when you make Soops or Broth for present Use, if it to be done softly, don't put much more Water than you intend to have Soop or Broth; and if you have the Convenience of an earthen Pan or Pipkin, and set on Wood Embers till it boils, then skim it, and put in your Seasoning; cover it close, and set it on Embers, so that it may do very softly for some Time, and both the Meat and Broths will be delicious. You must observe in all Broths and Soops, that one Thing does not taste more than another; but that the Taste be equal, and it has a fine agreeable Relish, according to what you design it for; and you must be sure, that all the Greens and Herbs you put in be cleaned, washed and picked.

Surbiton, Kingston, 1751

Soup

CUT in slices 3 or 4 lbs. coarse beef fry it quite brown in a small piece butter also fry 2 or 3 onions with the beef, when put in a stew pan add as much boiling water as you think sufficient add 3 carrots, 2 turnips, celery & a bunch of thyme, salt, pepper and cayenne, boil all together until quite tender, let it continue to simmer all day when strained add a table spoonful of catsup and a glass of sherry.

Roundhurst, Haslemere, 19th. Century

A Broth of Marybones

TAKE your Marrow bones and pare the flesh clean from them, & put as much sweet broth as will cover them, then take some mutton with a little suett & chop them fine with parsley, Tyme & Savoury, & put it to your bones, season with Salt, pepper, Cloves & Mace & serve it.

Loseley MS., Guildford, 17th. to 19th. Century (1379/80/1)

Eel Soup (Winter Soup - July to March)

½lb. Eel	mixed herbs (½ to be of Parsley)
1 Onion	2 pts. Water
5 Peppercorns & 2 Cloves	Salt & Pepper

Put clean, gutted & cut up Eel into a pan & all other ingredients simmer until liquid is reduced by half, Remove scum & strain, when cold skim off fat, Reheat when required.

Kingston Town, 19th. Century

ITEMS USED IN THE PREPARATION OF MEAT AND SOUPS

KEY (ITEMS ARE LISTED CLOCKWISE STARTING FROM 12 O'CLOCK):-

1 **Digestor or nineteenth-century Pressure Cooker.** A bone digestor was exhibited to the Royal Society by Denis Papin in 1680.

2 **Blue and White Pottery Dish** - a cottage example.

3 **Sycamore Plate.** Many ingredients such as Yeast were skimmed off and put on these plates to dry before storing.

4 **Brass Cat**, to hold a dish of food to keep warm in front of the fire. Two explanations are offered for its name - 'Cats sit by the fire and keep warm' or 'Whichever way you stand it , it will land on its feet'.

5 **An eighteenth-century Ladle.** Note the nib on the back of the handle to prevent it sliding into the dish and that both bowl and handle are in one piece..

6 **An eighteenth-century Kettle Holder,** the two sprung halves being made in sycamore and felt lined.

7 **A Strickle.** A wooden alternative to a Whetstone, used with bacon-fat and grit, which was kept in a horn.

8 **Two Forks,** one with a leather handle and one with a horn handle.

9 **Two nineteenth-century Food Choppers and a Chopping Bowl,** made from the solid.

10 **A Dish Slope,** use to tip dishes to ease ladelling out the gravy.

11 **A seventeenth-century Brass Skimmer,** generally paired with a brass ladle.

To make an Egg Soop

BEAT the Yolks of two Eggs in your Dish, with a Piece of Butter as big as a Hen's Egg, take a Tea Kettle of boiling Water in one Hand, and a Spoon in the other, pour in about a Quart by Degrees, then keep stirring it all the Time well till the Eggs are well mixed, and the Butter melted; then pour it into a Saucepan, and keep stirring it all the Time till it begins to simmer, take it off the Fire, and pour it between two Vessels, out of one into the other till it is quite smooth, and has a great Froth. Set it on the Fire again, keep stirring it till it is quite hot; then pour it into the Soop-dish, and send it to Table hot.

Surbiton, Kingston, 1751

To make Hare Soup

SKIN & wash Hare in warm water, & preserve the blood, cut it into small pieces, keep out the best parts of it, & put the remainder into a pan with 3 lbs of Beef, put the blood of the Hare into the pan also with some whole pipper onions & a bundle of sweet Herbs, Let it simmer for an hour stirring it occasionally. Strain it of from the above ingredients, & then add the other part of the Hare which was left out, some grated bread & salt, boil it 3 hours very slowly.

Loseley MS., Guildford, 17th. to 19th. Century. (1379/1/1)

To make Hodge-Podge*

TAKE a piece of beef, fat & lean together, about a lb, some pork a pound of Straig of mutton, cut into pieces, set it on the Fire, with two Quarts of water, an ounce of Barley, an Onion a little Bundle of Sweet Herbs, three or four Heads of Sellery wash clean & cut small, a little Mace, two or three Cloves, some Whole Pepper, tied all in a Muslin Rag, & put to the Meat three Turnips pared & cut in two, a large Carrot scraped clean & cut into sixpieces, a little Lettuce cut small, put all in a pot & cover it close. Let it stew very softly over a slow Fire five or six Hours; take out the Spice, Sweet Herbs & Onion, & pour all into a Soop-dish, and send it to Table; first season it with Salt. Half a pint of Green Peas, when it is the Season for them, is very good, If you let this boil fast it will waste too much; therefore you cannot do it too slow, if it does but simmer.

Rowtown, Chertsey, 19th. Century

Rhubarb Soup

3 pts of stock, 1 carrot, 1 onion, a few sticks of Rhubarb, cut into short lengths. Put the carrot & onion sliced fine & the rhubarb into the stock with a thin slice of bread & salt & pepper to taste bring to the boil & alow to simmer until the rhubarb is tender, strain heat up again serve with a slice of roasted bread.

Shere, 1897

---

*Hodge-Podge = Hotch-Potch = Hodge-Pot (*Oxford English Dictionary*)

To make a Turnip Soop

TAKE a Gallon of Water, & a bunch of Turnips, pare them, save three or four
out, put the rest in the Water with Half an Ounce of Whole Pepper, & an Onion
stuck with Cloves, a Blade of Mace, Half a Nutmeg bruised, a little Bundle of
Sweet Herbs, and a large Crust of Bread. Let these boil an Hour pretty fast, then
strain it through a Sieve, squeesing the Turnips through, wash and cut a bunch
of Sellery very small, set it in the Liquor on the Fire, cover it close, and let it
stew. In the mean Time cut the Turnips you saved into Dice, & two or three
small Carrots scraped clean, & cut into little Pieces; put Half these Turnips and
Carrots into the pot with the Sellery, & the other Half fry Brown in fresh Butter.
You must flour them first, and two or three onions peeled, cut in thin slices &
fry'd Brown; then put them all into the Soop, with an Ounze of Vermicella. Let
your Soop boil softly till the Sellery is quite tender, & your Soop good. Season it
with Salt to your Palate.

Surbiton, Kingston, 1751

Vegetable Soup

A knuckle of Veal and a shin of beef, put them in the stock pot, lay them close
together and cover with water, add 2 carrots, 2 turnips, 2 heads of celery, 2 large
onions, a bunch of chervil, and a little lemon thyme, boil it 6 hours, take out the
meat, strain the soup, put it in a cool place until you want it, when you must
take the fat off keeping the settlings at the bottom, add Indian soy anchovies & a
little cayenne. Put it in a stew pan get some lettice, chervil, and parsley washed,
and chop it up coarsely, give it a scald, cut carrot and turnip as for soup before
sent to table.

Roundhurst, Haslemere, 19th. Century

Watercress Soup

¼lb Watercress washed	1½lbs peeled potatoes
½lb onions	½lb Tomatoes
½pt milk	2pts white stock (preferably Chicken)
1 oz butter	nutmeg, salt & pepper

Put the sliced onions & potatoes into a pan, add stock & butter, cook gently
until soft. To serve add milk, pepper & salt, skin the tomatoes & chop up with
Watercress, add them to the pan together with the ground nutmeg, simmer a
further 10 to 15 minutes.

Abinger Hammer, *probably* 19th. Century

DIRECTIONS FOR THE SICK

To make Beef or Mutton Broth for very weak People who take but little Nourishment

TAKE a Pound of Beef, or Mutton, or both together: To a Pound put two Quarts of Water, first skin the Meat and take off all the Fat; then cut it into little Pieces, and boil it till it comes to a Quarter of a Pint. Season it with a very little Corn of Salt, skim off all the Fat, and give a Spoonful of this Broth at a Time. To very weak People, Half a Spoonful is enough; to some a Tea Spoonful at a Time; and to others a Tea-cup full. There is greater Nourishment from this than any Thing else.

Surbiton, Kingston, 1751

To make Bread-Soop for the Sick (or Panado)

TAKE a Quart of Water, set it on the Fire in a clean Saucepan, and as much dry Crust of Bread cut to pieces as the Top of a Penny-Loaf, the drier the better, a Bit of Butter as big as a Walnut; let it boil, then beat it with a Spoon, and keep boiling it till the Bread and Water is well mixed; then season it with a very little Salt, & it is a pretty thing for a weak Stomach.

Oxshott, 18th. Century

To make Buttered Water or what the Germans call Egg Soup & are very fond of it for Supper or Lent

TAKE a Pint of Water, beat up the Yolk of an Egg with the Water, put in a Piece of Butter as big as a small Walnut, two or three Nobs of Sugar, and keep stirring it all the Time it is on the Fire. When it begins to boil, bruise it between the Sauce-pan and a Mug till it is smooth, and has a great Froth; then itis fit to drink. This is ordered in a Cold, or where Egg will agree with the Stomach.

Surbiton, Kingston, 1751

Cows Milk next to Asses Milk, done thus

TAKE a Quart of Milk, set it in a Pan over Night, the next Morning take off all the Cream, then boil it and set it in the Pan again till Night; then skim it again, boil it, set it in the Pan again, and the next Morning skim it, warm it Blood-warm, and drink it as you do Asses Milk. It is very near as good, and with some consumptive People it is better.

Surbiton, Kingston, 1751

FISH

ON days when meat was forbidden, often a meal would start with pickled and smoked herring, brought from the coast ready done.

To broil Shrimp, Cod, Salmon, Whiting or Haddocks

FLOUR it, and have a quick clear Fire, set your Gridiron high, broil it of a fine Brown, lay it in your Dish, and for Sauce have good melted Butter. Take a Lobster, bruise the Body in the Butter, cut the Meat small, put all together into the melted Butter, make it hot and pour into your Dish, or into Basons. Garnish with Horse-raddish and Lemon.

Surbiton, Kingston, 1751

To dress little Fish

AS to all sorts of little Fish, such as Smelts, Roch, &c. they should be fry'd dry and of a fine Brown, and nothing but plain Butter. Garnish with Lemon.

And to boiled Salmon the same, only garnish with Lemon and Horse-raddish.

And with all boiled Fish, you should put a good deal of Salt and Horse-raddish in the Water; except Mackrel, with which put Salt and Mint, Parsley and Fennel, which you must chop to put into the Butter, and some love scalded Gooseberries with them. And be sure to boil your Fish well; but take great Care they don't break.

Surbiton, Kingston, 1751

Forcemeat for various kinds of Fish

FOR each mackerel 1 pounded anchovy, 1 egg yolk, 1 table spoonful of chopped parsley, 1 oz butter, ¼ cup fresh breadcrumbs, squeeze of lemon juice & a tiny pinch of cayenne. Melt the butter and mix all together.

Epsom, 1857

To fry Carp

FIRST scale and gut them, wash them clean, lay them in a Cloth to dry, then flour them, and fry them of a fine light Brown. Fry some Toast cut Three-corner-ways, and the Rows; when your Fish is done, lay them on a coarse Cloth to drain. Let your sauce be Butter and Anchovy, with the juice of Lemon. Lay your Carp in the Dish, the Rows on each side, and garnish with the fry'd Toast and Lemon.

Surbiton, Kingston, 1751

To fry Eels

MAKE them very clean, cut them into Pieces, season them with Pepper and Salt, flour them and fry them in Butter. Let your Sauce be plain Butter melted, with the Juice of Lemon. Be sure they be well drained from the Fat before you lay them in the Dish.

Surbiton, Kingston, 1751

Eels Boiled

4 small eels, sufficient water to cover them; a large bunch of parsley. Mode, choose small eels for boiling; put them in a stewpan with the parsley, & just sufficient water to cover them; simmer till tender, take them out pour a little butter & parsley over them, & serve some in a tureen.

Epsom, 1850-60

To broil Haddocks when they are in High Season

SCALE them, gut and wash them clean, don't rip open their Bellies, but take the Guts out with the Gills, dry them in a clean Cloth very well: If there be any Row or Liver take it out, but put it in again; flour them well, and have a clear good Fire. Let your Gridiron be hot and clean, lay them on, turn them quick two or three Times for fear of sticking; then let one Side be enough and turn the other Side. When that is done, lay them in your Dish, and have plain Butter in a Cup.

They eat finely salted a Day or two before you dress them, and hung up to dry, or boiled with Egg-Sauce. *Newcastle* is a famous Place for salted Haddocks. They come in Barrels, and keep a great while.

Surbiton, Kingston, 1751

To dress Herring and Cabbage

BOIL your Cabbage tender, then put it in a Sauce-pan, and chop it with a Spoon; put in a good Piece of Butter, let it stew, stirring lest it should burn. Take some Red Herrings and split them open, and toast them before the Fire till they are hot through. Lay the Cabbage in a Dish and lay the Herring on it, and send it to the Table hot.

Or pick your Herring from the Bones, and throw all over your Cabbage. Have ready a hot Iron, and just hold it over the Herring to make it hot, and send it away quick.

Surbiton, Kingston, 1751

How to dress Mackroll au Maitre d'Hotel

SPLIT but not divide it, then completely broil, browning it. Have a dish quite hot, & have ready Parsley, Charvel & Spring Onions all cut fine as possible. When the fish is broiled, open and put these herbs raw, with a large lump of butter, over which squeeze half a lemon to oil the butter & pour over.

Losely MS., Guildford, 17th. to 19th. Centuries.

To pickle or bake Mackrel, to keep all the Year

GUT them, cut off their Heads, cut them open, dry them very well with a clean
Cloth, take a Pan which they will lie cleaverly in, lay a few Bay-Leaves at the
Bottom, rub the Bone with a little Bay-salt beat fine, take a little beaten Mace, a
few Cloves beat fine, Black and White Pepper beat fine; mix a little Salt, rub
them inside and out with the Spice, lay them in a Pan, and between every Lay of
the Mackrel put a few Bay-Leaves, then cover them with Vinegar, tie them
down close with Brown Paper, put them in a slow Oven; they will take a good
while doing; when they are enough, uncover them, let them stand till cold, then
pour away all that Vinegar, and put as much good Vinegar as will cover them,
and put in an Onion stuck with Cloves. Send them to the Oven again, let them
stand two Hours in a very slow Oven, and they will keep all the Year; but you
must not put in your Hands to take out the Mackrel, if you can avoid it, but
take a Slice to take them out with. The great Bones of the Mackrel taken out
and broiled, is a pretty little Plate to fill up a Corner of a Table.

Surbiton, Kingston, 1751

To pot Lamphreys

SKIN them, cleanse them with Salt, and then wipe them dry; beat some Black
Pepper, Mace and Cloves, mix them with Salt and season them. Lay them in a
Pan, and cover them with clarified Butter. Bake them an Hour; let them be
seasoned, and one will be enough for a Pot. You must season them well, let your
Butter be good, and they will keep a long Time.

Surbiton, Kingston, 1751

Salmon in Cases

CUT your Salmon into little Pieces, such as will lay rolled in Half Sheets of
Paper. Season it with Pepper, Salt and Nutmeg; butter the Inside of the Paper
well, fold the Paper so as nothing can come out, then lay them on a Tin Plate to
be baked, pour a little melted Butter over the Papers, and then Crumbs of Bread
all over them. Don't let your Oven be too hot, for fear of burning the Paper. A
Tin Oven before the Fire does best. When you think they are enough, serve
them up just as they are. There will be Sauce enough in the Papers.

Surbiton, Kingston, 1751

To Pot Salmon

TAKE a Piece of fresh Salmon, scale it and wipe it clean (let your Piece, or
Pieces, be as big as will lie cleaverly on your Pot) season it with *Jamaica* Pepper,
Black Pepper, Mace and Cloves beat fine, mix'd with Salt, a little Sal Prunella*
beat fine and rub the Bone with. Season with a little of the Spice, pour clarified
Butter over it, and bake it well. Then take it out carefully, and lay it to drain;
when cold, season it well, lay it in your Pot close, and cover it with clarified
Butter. Thus you may do Carp, Tench,Trout, and several Sorts of Fish.

Surbiton, Kingston, 1751

* Sal Prunella = fused Nitre (Potassium Nitrate).

13

To make Shrimp Sauce

TAKE a Pint of Beef Gravy, and Half a Pint of Shrimps, thicken it with a good Piece of Butter rolled in Flour. Let the Gravy be well seasoned and let it boil.

Surbiton, Kingston, 1751

Pickle for Sturgeon

TAKE 3 pints of water let it boyle fast in a little Salt, let them boil together, it must be throughly cold, and put in a little of the best Vinegar for pickle for Sturgeon.

Losely MS., Guildford, 17th. to 19th. Centuries.

To Fricafsee Turbot

TAKE a Turbut - skin it and cut into small slices. Dip it into a batter, made as always, Eggs Cream, Mace and Nutmeg to tast and bind with any flower water you please. Then brown fry the pieces, and serve with Forst Meat balls and fish sauce, serve with Mushrooms and Oysters all fried and around.

Chertsey, 18th. Century

To make Water-Sokey

TAKE some of the smallest Plaise or Flounders you can get, wash them clean, cut the Fins close, put them into a Stew-pan, put just Water enough to boil them in, a little Salt and a Bunch of Parsley; when they are enough, send them to Table in a Soop-Dish, with the Liquor to keep them hot. Have Parsley and Butter in a Cup.

Surbiton, Kingston, 1751

Salt Fish Pie

SOAK salt fish overnight, simmer in fresh water until cooked, take away the skin & bones, & fork over the fish. Take ½lb. (to 2lbs. of fish) white bread crumbs boiled in 1 gill of milk, add fresh ¼lb. butter & a handfull of parsley cut fine, nutmeg, mustard & pepper to taste, put all ingredients into dish cover & cook in bread oven 1 hour. A pastry cover can be added if liked.

Rowtown, Chertsey, 19th. Century

MEAT

IN LARGE HOUSEHOLDS, carving was done by a knight, without a fork, and supposedly not touching the meat with his left hand, the best slice immediately sent to his Lord. In smaller houses the hostess carved the spit-roasted joint, until the middle of the eighteenth century. In 1830 there was a school in London to teach young ladies to carve. That a man carves is only a tradition of the last hundred years.

BEEF

IF Beef, be sure to paper the Top, and baste it well all the Time it is roasting, and throw a Handful of Salt on it. When you see the Smoke draw to the Fire, it is near enough; then take off the Paper, baste it well, and drudge it with a little Flour to make a fine Froth. Never salt your roast Meat before you lay it to the Fire, for that draws out all the Gravy. If you would keep it a few Days before you dress it, dry it very well with a clean Cloth, then flour it all over, and hang it where the Air will come to it; but be sure always to mind that there is no damp Place about it, if there is, you must dry it well with a Cloth. Take up your Meat, and garnish your Dish with nothing but Horse-raddish.

Surbiton, Kingston, 1751

Beef Escarlot

TAKE a Briscuit of Beef, Half a Pound of coarse Sugar, two Ounces of Bay Salt, a Pound of common Salt, mix all together and rub the Beef, lay it in an earthen Pan, and turn it every Day. It may lie a Fortnight in the Pickle, then boil it, and serve it up either with Savoys, or a Pease Pudding.

Note, It eats much finer cold, cut into Slices, and sent to Table.

Surbiton, Kingston, 1751

Roast Beef that equals Hare

TAKE the inside of a large sirloin, soak it in a glass of port wine & a glass of vinegar mixed for 48 hours, have ready a very fine stuffing & bind it up tight. Roast it over a hanging spit & baste it with a glass of port, & one of vinegar & a teaspoon of pounded all spice, larding improves the look and flavour. Serve with a rich gravy in the dish, Currant jelly & melted butter in tureens.

Chipstead, 1850

To make Hunter's Beef

6lbs of lean beef boiled until tender, beat it fine in a mortar, add 2lbs of clarified butter, 2 nutmegs pepper and salt, beat it all well together put it in pots with clarified butter run over. Colour it with cochineal.

Roundhurst, Haslemere, 19th. Century

To stew Larded Beef

MIX some Salt & Peper, cut some Bacon in long slices role your Bacon in the Salt & Peper, then make a hole threw your Beef & put your Bacon in; put about a pint of Water in your stewpan with a little Alspice, a few Cloves and a few Whole Pepper then put in your Beef & set it on the fire the Night before turn it in the Morning take care it does very slow all the time.

Epsom, after 1798

A Pretty Side-Dish of Beef

ROAST a tender Piece of Beef, lay fat Bacon all over it and roll it in Paper; baste it, and when it is roasted cut about two Pounds in thin Slices, lay them into a Stew-pan, and take six large Cucumbers, peel them and chop them small, lay over them a little Pepper and Salt, stew them in Butter for about ten Minutes, then drain out the Butter, and shake some Flour over them; toss them up, pour in Half a Pint of Gravy, let them stew till they are thick, and dish them up.

Surbiton, Kingston, 1751

To Fry Beef Steaks

TAKE Rump Steaks, beat them very well with a Roller, fry them in Half a Pint of Ale that is not bitter, and whilst they are frying, cut a large Onion small, a very little Thyme, some Parsley shred small, some grated Nutmeg, and a little Pepper and Salt; roll all together in a Piece of Butter, and then in a little Flour, put this into the Stew-pan, and shake all together. When the Steaks are tender, and the Sauce of a fine Thickness, dish it up.

Surbiton, Kingston, 1751

Another Way to do Beef Steaks

CUT your Steaks, Half broil them, then lay them into a Stew-pan, season them with Pepper and Salt, just cover them with Gravy, and a Piece of Butter rolled in Flour. Let them stew for Half an Hour, beat up the Yolks of two Eggs, stir all together for two or three Minutes, and then serve it up.

Surbiton, Kingston, 1751

FOR THE DINING TABLE

KEY: (ITEMS ARE LISTED FROM LEFT TO RIGHT)

1   **Eighteenth-century Mahogany Cheese Cradle.** This takes a wedge from a circular cheese, placed so that its rim is downwards.

2   **Mahogany Punch Ladle**

3   **Eighteenth-century Mahogany Knife Box.**

4   **Victorian Mahogany Decanter Coaster,** mounted on castors so that it could be pushed clockwise to the diner on the left.

5   **Nineteenth-century Mahogany Wine Carrier,** for four bottles, placed corks outwards. Note the semicircular cut out at each end to take the bottle necks.

6   **Silver Wine Strainer.**

Savoury Liver

½lb. Liver (cut into 4)	4 Tablespoonfuls bread crumbs
4 pieces of bacon	1 Desertspoonful chopped parsley
½pt. gravy	Salt & pepper

Put liver in baking dish, just cover with gravy, mix breadcrumbs with parsley salt & pepper, & cover liver slices & then bacon on top, cover dish & bake moderate oven for ½ hr., remove cover crisp bacon & serve with remainder of gravy.

Dorking Town, 19th. Century

To Stew Neats Tongues Whole

TAKE two Tongues, let them stew in Water just to cover them for two Hours, then peel them, put them in again with a Pint of strong Gravy, Half a Pint of White Wine, a Bundle of Sweet Herbs, a little Pepper and Salt, some Mace, Cloves, and Whole Pepper ty'd in a Muslin Rag, a Spoonful of Capers chopp'd, Turnips and Carrots sliced, and a Piece of Butter roll'd in Flour; let all stew together very softly over a slow Fire for two Hours, then take out the Spice and Sweet Herbs, and send it to Table. You may leave out the Turnips and Carrots, or boil them by themselves, and lay them in the Dish, just as you like.

Surbiton, Kingston, 1751

To boyle Tripes

TAKE a little sweet broath onions & parsley chopped small take a little Mustard some Sugar Vinegar and a little pepper.

Losely MS., Guildford, 17th. to 19th. Centuries. (1379/80/1)

TRIPE may be dressed in a variety of ways; it may be cut into pieces & fried in batter, stewed in gravy with mushrooms or cut up into collops, sprinkled with minced onions & savoury herbs, & fried a nice brown in clarified butter.

Epsom, 1850/60

MUTTON AND LAMB

ALMOST every city had a different method of dressing* the carcase. Surrey generally followed the simple London method, avoiding skewering and not doubling one part over another, so as not to spoil the meat, & help to keep it longer.

Epsom, 1850/60

* dressing = cutting up

Mutton

A Leg of Mutton of six Pounds will take an Hour at a quick Fire; if frosty Weather as Hour and a Quarter; nine Pounds, an Hour and a Half; a Leg of twelve Pounds will take two Hours; if frosty, two Hours and a Half; a large Saddle of Mutton will take three Hours, because of papering it; a small Saddle will take an Hour and a Half, and so on, according to the Size; a Breast will take Half an Hour at a quick Fire; a Neck, if large, an Hour; if very small, little better than Half an Hour; a Shoulder much about the same Time as the Leg.

Surbiton, Kingston, 1751

To Bake Lamb and Rice

TAKE a Neck and Loin of Lamb, half roast it, take it up, cut it into Steaks, then take Half a Pound of Rice, put it into a Quart of good Gravy, with two or three Blades of Mace, and a little Nutmeg. Do it over a Stove of slow Fire till the Rice begins to be thick; then take it off, stir in a Pound of Butter, and when that is quite melted stir in the Yolks of six Eggs, first beat; then take a Dish and butter it all over, take the Steaks and put a little Pepper and Salt over them, dip them in a little melted Butter, lay them into the Dish, pour the Gravy which comes out of them over them, and then the Rice, beat the Yolks of three Eggs and pour all over, send it to the Oven, and bake it better than Half an Hour.

Surbiton, Kingston, 1751

To boyle Mutton

TAKE Strong Broath of the boyling of other Mutton and straine it through a strainer then take Spinnage and Skalions* cut 2 Inches long and a peice of sweet butter some and some other little sweet herbes chopped very small and some whole Cloves and Mace.

Losely MS., Guildford, 17th. to 19th. Centuries. (1379/80/1)

To Force a Leg of Lamb

WITH a sharp Knife carefully take out all the Meat, and leave the Skin whole and the Fat on it, make the Lean you cut into Force-Meat thus: To two Pounds of Meat, three Pounds of Beef Sewet cut fine, and beat in a Marble Mortar till it is very fine, and take away all the Skin of the Meat and Sewet, then mix it with four Spoonfuls of grated Bread, eight or ten Cloves, five or six large Blades of Mace dry'd and beat fine, Half a large Nutmeg grated, a little Pepper and Salt, a little Lemon-peel cut fine, a very little Thyme, some Parsley, and four Eggs: Mix all together, put into the Skin again just as it was, in the same Shape, sew it up, roast it baste it with Butter, cut the Loin into Steaks and fry it nicely, lay the Leg in the Dish and the Loin round it with stew'd Cauliflower all round upon the Loin, pour a Pint of good Gravy into the Dish, and send it to Table. If you don't like the Cauliflower, it may be omitted.

Surbiton, Kingston, 1751

* Scallions are elongated onions which fail to bulb (not unlike Welsh Onions).

A Harico of Mutton

TAKE a Neck or Loin of Mutton, cut it into six Pieces, flour it and fry it Brown on both Sides in the Stew-pan, then pour out all the Fat; put in some Turnips and Carrots cut like Dice, two Dozen of Chesnuts blanched, two or three Lettuces cut small, six little round Onions, a Bundle of Sweet Herbs, some Pepper and Salt, and two or three Blades of Mace; cover it close, and let it stew for an Hour, then take off the Fat and dish it up.

Surbiton, Kingston, 1751

To make Mutton Hash

WHEN you roast a leg of Mutton put the gravy in a basin when it comes from the table and save it. Then cut the mutton in thin slices, and put it with the gravy in a saucepan and let it simmer over the fire, but not to boil, put in a little sliced pickled gherkins and pepper and salt, to taste, with Reading sauce.

Roundhurst, Haslemere, 19th. Century

A Neck of Mutton, call'd, The Hasty Dish

TAKE a large Pewter or Silver Dish, made like a deep Soop Dish, with an Edge about an Inch deep on the Inside, on which the Lid fixes (with a Handle at Top) so fast that you may lift it up full, by that Handle without falling. This Dish is call'd a Necromancer. Take a Neck of Mutton about six Pounds, take off the skin, cut it into Chops, not too thick, slice a French Roll, thin, peel and slice a very large Onion, pare and slice three or four Turnips, lay a Row of Mutton in the Dish, on that a Row of Roll, then a Row of Turnips, and then Onions, a little Salt, then the Meat, and so on; put in a little Bundle of Sweet Herbs, and two or three Blades of Mace; have a Tea Kettle of Water boiling, fill the Dish and cover it close, hang the Dish on the Back of two Chairs by the Rim, have ready three Sheets of Brown Paper, tare each Sheet into five Pieces, and draw them through your hand, light one Piece and hold it under the Bottom of the Dish, moving the Paper about; as fast as the Paper burns light another till all is burnt, and your meat will be enough. Fifteen Minutes just does it. Send it to Table hot in the Dish.

Note, This Dish was first contrived by Mr. Rich, and is much admired by the Nobility.

Surbiton, Kingston, 1751

To Stuff a Shoulder of Mutton

TAKE half a hundred of oysters and shrid y^u grate a little nuttmeg & a little s-ett margoram a little lemon peele time finely shrid y^u grate a little bread y^u take y^r yolk of an egg & mix it all together cut a hole under y^r knocal & stuff it in for some good gravey Serve oisters stewed in it & their own lickle.

Farnham, 18th. Century

Kidneys

TAKE as many as you wish for, broil* them until brown then put them into the stew-pan with some thick gravy, & let them stew until quite tender. Add a teaspoonful of mustard, some ketchup & Guildford sauce.

Losely MS., Guildford, 17th. to 19th. Centuries. (1379/109)

Lambs Fry

1 lb. Lambs Fry	3 pints of water
1 Egg	1 teaspoonful chopped Parsley
Bread crumbs	Salt and Pepper

Boil Fry in water, take out and dry, mix grated bread crumbs, season well, brush the fry with egg yolk & sprinkle crumbs over, fry for five minutes serve, hot with parsley.

Epsom, 1850/60

PORK

Wild boar was considered better flavoured than pig and was served to Royalty. Surrey cottagers, in common with other parts of the country until the late nineteenth century, kept two pigs, one paid the annual rent while the other fed the family.

Pork

PORK must be well done, or it is apt to Surfeit. When you roast a Loin take a sharp Pen-Knife and cut the skin across, to make the Crackling eat better. The Chine you must not cut at all. The best Way to roast a Leg, is first to parboil it, then skin it and roast it; baste it with Butter, then take a little Sage, shred it fine, a little Pepper and Salt, a little Nutmeg and a few Crumbs of Bread, throw these over it all the Time it is roasting, then have a little Drawn Gravey to put in the Dish the Crumbs that drop from it. Some love the Knuckle stuffed with Onions and Sage shred small, with a little Pepper and Salt, Gravy and Apple Sauce to it. This they call a Mock Goose. The Spring, or Hand of Pork, if very young, roasted like a Pig, eats very well, otherwise it is better boiled. The Sparerib should be basted with a little Bit of Butter, a very little Dust of Flour and some Sage shred small; but we never make any Sauce to it but Apple Sauce. The best Way to dress Pork Griskins is to roast them, baste them with a little Butter and Crumbs of Bread, Sage and a little Pepper and Salt. Few eat anything with them but Mustard.

Surbiton, Kingston, 1751

* To broil = to burn [grill] (1568) = to cook meat on a grid iron over fire (1634)
Oxford English Dictionary

Roast Belly of Pork with Sage and Onions

2 Rashers, 2 Potatoes and 1 Onion for each person, Sage and Pepper.
Peal and halve onions, slice potatoes and parboil both, mix and place half of the mixture in a dish, sprinkle with chopped sage and pepper, place the rashers on top and cover with the mixture, finish in front of fire. [This was a cheap meal for farm workers].

Rowtown, Chertsey, 19th. Century

To boil Pickled Pork

BE sure you put it in when the Water boils. If a middling Piece, an Hour will boil it; if a very large Piece, an Hour and a Half, or two Hours. If you boil pickled Pork too long it will go to a Jelly.

Surbiton, Kingston, 1751

To dress a Loin of Pork with Onions

TAKE a Fore-Loin of Pork, and roast it as at another Time, peel a Quarrer of a Peck of Onions, and slice them thin, lay them in the Dripping-pan, which must be very clean, under the Pork, let the Fat drop on them; when the Pork is nigh enough, put the Onions into the Sauce-pan, let them simmer over the Fire a Quarter of an Hour, shaking them well, then pour out all the Fat as well as you can, shake in a very little Flour, a Spoonful of Vinegar, and three Tea Spoonfuls of Mustard, shake all well together, and stir in the Mustard, set it over the Fire for four or five Minutes, lay the Pork in a Dish, and the Onions in a Bason. This is an admirable Dish to those who love Onions.

Surbiton, Kingston, 1751

To Stuff a Chine of Pork.

MAKE a Stuffing of the Fat Leaf of Pork, Parsley, Thyme, Sage, Eggs, Crumbs of Bread, season it with Pepper, Salt, Shallot and Nutmeg, and stuff it thick; then roast it gently, and when it is about a Quarter roasted, cut the Skin in Slips, and make your Sauce with Apples, Lemon-peel, two or three Cloves, and a Blade of Mace; sweeten it with Sugar, put some Butter in it, and have Mustard in a Cup.

Surbiton, Kingston, 1751

To Boil a Ham

WHEN you boil a Ham, put it into a Copper, if you have one; let it be about three or four Hours before it boils, and keep it well skim'd all the Time; then, if it is a small one, one Hour and a Half will boil it, after the Copper begins to boil; and, if a large one, two Hours will do; for you are to consider the Time it has been heating in the Water, which softens the Ham, and makes it boil the sooner.

Surbiton, Kingston, 1751

o dress a Ham à la Braise

CLEAR the Knuckle, take of the Swerd, and lay it in Water to freshen; then tie it about with a String, take Slices of Bacon and Beef, beat and season them well with Spice and Sweet Herbs; then lay them in the Bottom of a Kettle with Onions, Parsnips, and Carrots sliced, with some Cives* and Parsley: Lay in your Ham the Fat Side uppermost, and cover it with slices of Beef, and over that slices of Bacon, then lay on some sliced Roots and Herbs, the same as under it: Cover it close, and stop it close with Paste, put Fire both over and under it, and let it stew with a very slow Fire twelve Hours; put it in a Pan, drudge it well with grated Bread, and Brown it with a hot Iron; then serve it up on a clean Napkin, garnished with raw Parsley.

Note, If you eat it hot, make a Ragoo thus: Take a Veal Sweetbread, some Livers of Fowls, Cocks-Combs, Mushrooms and Truffles, toss them up in a Pint of good Gravy season with Spice as you like, thicken it with a Piece of Butter rolled in Flour, and a Glass of Red Wine; then Brown your Ham as above, and let it stand a Quarter of an Hour to drain the Fat out; take the Liquor it was stew'd in, strain it, skim all the Fat off, put it to the Gravy, and boil it up. It will do as well as the Essence of Ham. Sometimes you may serve it up with a Ragoo of Craw-Fish, and sometimes with Carp Sauce.

Surbiton, Kingston, 1751

Ham Loaf

1 lb. cooked ham (¼ Fat)	1 glass milk
2 oz. bread	1 egg
parsley	ground mace - pepper

Mince ham, pour boiling milk on bread, mix and season, add beaten egg. Grease mould, press mixture down, bake in medium oven until brown.

Rowtown, Chertsey, 19th. Century

HARE, RABBIT & VENISON

A hare in cold weather will remain good for 10 to 14 days, care must be taken to prevent the inside from becoming musty. With few exceptions, game depends almost entirely for the fine flavour and tenderness of its flesh, on the time which it is allowed to hang before it is cooked, and is never good when very fresh.

Abridged from Eliza Acton, 1855

A Hare

YOU must have a quick Fire. If it be a small Hare, put three Pints of Milk and a Half a Pound of fresh Butter in the Dripping-pan, which must be very clean and nice; if a large one, two Quarts of Milk and Half a Pound of fresh Butter. You must baste your Hare well with this all the Time it is roasting, and when the Hare has soak'd up all the Butter and Milk it will be enough.

Surbiton, Kingston, 1751

* Cives = Chives (*Oxford English Dictionary*)

23

Hare Broiled, a Supper or Luncheon Dish

LEGS and shoulders of a roast hare, cayenne and salt to taste, butter. Cut the legs and shoulders of a roast hare, season highly with cayenne and salt, broil them over a very clear fire for 5 minutes, dish them onto a hot dish & send to table quickly.

Epsom, 1850/60

To do a Hare

WITH time & onion & parsley Shrid & Strowed over hare as he is rosting y^u bast him in milk.

Farnham, 18th. Century

A Jugged Hare

CUT it into little Pieces, lard them here and there with little Slips of Bacon, season them with a very little Pepper and Salt, put them in an earthen Jugg, with a Blade or two of Mace, an Onion stuck with Cloves, and a Bundle of Sweet Herbs; cover the Jugg or Jar you do it in, so close that nothing can get in, then set it in a Pot of boiling Water, keep the Water boiling, and three Hours will do it; then turn it out into the Dish, and take out the Onion and Sweet Herbs, and send it to Table hot. If you don't like it larded, leave it out.

Surbiton, Kingston, 1751

To boil Rabbits

TRUSS them for Boiling, boil them quick and white: For Sauce take the Livers, boil and shred them, and some Parsley shred fine, and pickled Astertion-Buds chopped fine, or Capers; mix these with Half a Pint of good Gravy, a Glass of White Wine, a little beaten Mace and Nutmeg, a little Pepper and Salt if wanted, a Piece of Butter as big as a large Walnut rolled in Flour; let it all boil together till it is thick, take up the Rabbits and pour the Sauce over them. Garnish with Lemon. You may lard them with Bacon, if it is liked.

Surbiton, Kingston, 1751

Conyns in Greke Wine

CONYNS should be fully grown. One Coney [portioned] flour pepper salt Basil finely minced, mix Sweet red wine from Greece, half a pint, 6 ounces of dried grapes [raisons], 6 ounces dried apricots, a little powdered cloves, 12 crushed juniper berries, some thyme and leave overnight. Next day pour this over the portions of Coney. The next day dry the meat and roll it in the flour and basil, fry it lightly. Put back into liquid and simmer for three parts of an hour. Remove meat and reduce liquid to thick, pour over meat.

Haslemere Town, 1399

To dress Rabbits in Casserole

DIVIDE the Rabbits into Quarters. You may lard them or let them alone, just as you please, shake some Flour over them, and fry them with Lard or Butter, then put them into an earthen Pipkin with a Quart of good Broth, a Glass of White Wine, a little Pepper and Salt, if wanted, a Bunch of Sweet Herbs, and a Piece of Butter as big as a Walnut rolled in Flour; cover them close and let them stew Half an Hour, then dish them up and pour the Sauce over them. Garnish with *Seville* Orange cut into thin slices and notched; the Peel that is cut out lay prettily between the Slices.

Surbiton, Kingston, 1751

To Roast a Rabbit, Hare Fashion

LARD a Rabbit with Bacon; roast it as you do a Hare, and it eats very well. But then you must make Gravy-Sauce; but if you don't lard it, White-Sauce.

Surbiton, Kingston, 1751

To Boil a Haunch or Neck of Venison

LAY it in Salt for a Week, then boil it in a Cloth well flour'd; for every Pound of Venison, allow a Quarter of an Hour for the boiling. For Sauce you must boil some Cauliflowers, pull'd into little Sprigs in Milk and Water, some fine White Cabbage, some Turnips cut into Dice, with some Beet-root cut into long narrow Pieces about an Inch and a Half long, and Half an Inch thick: Lay a Sprig of Cauliflower, and some of the Turnips mashed with some Cream and a little Butter; Let your Cabbage be boiled, and then beat in a Sauce-pan with a Piece of Butter and Salt, lay that next the Cauliflower, then the Turnips, then the Cabbage, and so on, till the Dish is full; place the Beet-root here and there, just as you fancy; it looks very pretty and is a fine Dish. Have a little melted Butter in a Cup if wanted.

Note, A Leg of Mutton cut Venison Fashion, and dress'd the same Way is a pretty Dish: Or a fine Neck, with the Scraig cut off. This eats well broil'd or hash'd, with Gravy and Sweet-Sauce the next Day.

Surbiton, Kingston, 1751

To Roast Venison

TAKE a Haunch of Venison, and spit it. Take four Sheets of white Paper, butter them well, and roll about your Venison, then tye your Paper on with a small String, and baste it well all the Time it is Roasting. If your Fire is very good and brisk, two hours will do it; and, if a small Haunch, an Hour and a Half. The Neck and Shoulder must be done in the same Manner, which will take an Hour and a Half, and when it is enough take off the Paper, and drudge it with a little Flour, just to make a Froth; but you must be very quick, for fear the Fat should melt. You must not put any Sauce in the Dish, but what comes out of the Meat, but have some very good Gravy and put it in your Sauce Boat or Bason. You must always have Sweet-Sauce with your Venison in another Bason. If it is a large Haunch it will take two Hours and a Half.   Surbiton, Kingston, 1751

25

Different Sorts of Sauce for Venison

YOU may tke either of these Sauces for Venison. Currant Jelly warm'd; or Half a Pint of Red Wine, with a Quarter of a Pound of Sugar, simmer'd over a clear Fire for five or six Minutes; or half a Pint of Vinegar, and a Quarter of a Pound of Sugar, simmer'd till it is a Syrup.

Surbiton, Kingston, 1751

FOWLS & GAME BIRDS

Fowls

A Large Fowl, three Quarters of an Hour; a middling one, Half an Hour;; very small Chickens, twenty Minutes. Your Fire must be very quick and clear when you lay them down.

Surbiton, Kingston, 1751

Directions concerning Poultry

IF your Fire is not very quick and clear when you lay your Poultry down to roast, it will not eat near so sweet, or look so beautiful to the Eye.

Surbiton, Kingston, 1751

To pull a Chicken for the Sick

YOU must take as much cold Chicken as you think proper, take off the Skin and pull the Meat into little Bits as thick as a Quill, then take the Bones, boil them with a little Salt till they are good. Strain it; then take a Spoonful of the Liquor, a Spoonful of Milk, a little Bit of Butter as big as a large Nutmeg rolled in Flour, a little Chopped Parsley, as much as will lye on a Sixpence, and a little Salt if wanted. This will be enough for half a small Chicken. Put all together in a Sauce-pan; then keep shaking it till it is thick and pour into a hot Plate.

Oxshott, 18th. Century

A pretty Way of stewing Chickens

TAKE two fine Chickens, Half boil them, then take them up in a Pewter or Silver Dish, if you have one; cut up your Fowls, and separate all the Joint-Bones one from another, and then take out the Breast-Bones. If there is not Liquor enough from the Fowls add a few Spoonfuls of the Water they were boil'd in, put in a Blade of Mace, and a little Salt; cover it close with another Dish, set it over a Stove or Chaffing-dish of Coals, let it stew till the Chickens are enough, and then send them hot to the Table in the same Dish they were stew'd in.

   Note, This is a very pretty Dish for any sick Person, or for a lying-in Lady. For Change it is better than Butter, and the Sauce is very agreeable and pretty.

   N.B. You may do Rabbits, Partridges, or more Game this Way.

Surbiton, Kingston, 1751

Chickens with Tongues. A good Dish for a great deal of Company

TAKE six small Chickens boiled very White, six Hogs Tongues boiled and peeled, a Cauliflower boiled very White in Milk and Water whole, and a good eal of Spinach boiled Green; then lay your Cauliflower in the Middle, the Chickens close all round, and the Tongues round them with the Roots outwards, and the Spinach in little Heaps between the Tongues. Garnish with little Pieces of Bacon toasted, and lay a little Bit on each of the Tongues.

Surbiton, Kingston, 1751

Directions for Geese and Ducks

AS to Geese and Ducks, you should have some Sage shred fine, and a little Pepper and Salt, and put them into the Belly; but never put any Thing into Wild Ducks.

Surbiton, Kingston, 1751

To Roast a Green Goose with Green Sauce

ROAST your goose nicely, in the meantime make your sauce thus; take half a pint of the juice of sorrel, a spoonful of white wine, a little grated nutmeg, and some grated bread; boil this over a gentle fire, and sweeten it with pounded sugar to your taste, let your goose have a good froth on it before you take it up, put some good strong gravy in the dish, and the same in a boat. Garnish with lemon.

Dormansland, 18th. Century

To Roast Geese, Turkies, &c.

WHEN you roast a Goose, Turky, or Fowls of any Sort, take care to singe them with a Piece of white Paper, and baste them with a Piece of Butter; drudge them with a little Flour, and when the Smoke begins to draw to the Fire, and they look plump, baste them again, and drudge them with a little Flour, and take them up.

Surbiton, Kingston, 1751

Ducks à la Mode

TAKE two fine Ducks, cut them into Quarters, fry them in Butter a little Brown, then pour out all the Fat, and throw a little Flour over them; add Half a Pint of good Gravy, a Quarter of a Pint of Red Wine, two Shalots, an Anchovy, and a Bundle of Sweet Herbs; cover them close, and let them stew a Quarter of an Hour; take out the Herbs, skim off the Fat, and let your Sauce be as thick as Cream. Send it to Table, and garnish with Lemon.

Surbiton, Kingston, 1751

27

To dress a Duck with Cucumbers

TAKE three or four Cucumbers, pare them, take out the Seeds, cut them into little Pieces, lay them in Vinegar for two or three Hours before, with two large Onions peeled and sliced, then do your Duck as above; then take the Duck out, and put in the Cucumbers and Onions, first drain them in a Cloth, let them be a little Brown, shake a little Flour over them, in the mean Time let your Duck be stewing in the Sauce-pan with Half a Pint of Gravy for a Quarter of an Hour, then add to it the Cucumbers and Onions, with Pepper and Salt to your Palate, a good Piece of Butter rolled in Flour, and two or three Spoonfuls of Red Wine; shake all together, and let it stew together for eight or ten Minutes, then take up your Duck and pour the Sauce over it.

Or you may roast your Duck, and make this Sauce and pour over it, but then a Quarter of a Pint of Gravy will be enough.

Surbiton, Kingston, 1751

To dress a Wild Duck the best Way

FIRST Half roast it, then lay it in a Dish, carve it, but leave the Joints hanging together, throw a little Pepper and Salt, and squeeze the juice of a Lemon over it, turn it on the Breast, and press it hard with a Plate, then add to it its own Gravy, and two or three Spoonfuls of good Gravy; cover it close with another Dish, and set it over a Stove ten Minutes, then send it to Table hot in the Dish it was done in, and garnish with Lemon. You may add a little Red Wine, and a Shalot cut small, if you like it, but it is apt to make the Duck eat hard, unless you first heat the Wine and pour it in just as it is done.

Surbiton, Kingston, 1751

To Roast Partridges

LET them be nicely roasted but not too much, drudge them with a little Flour, and baste them moderately, let them have a fine Froth, let there be good Gravy-Sauce in the Dish and Bread-Sauce in Basons, made thus: Take a Pint of Water, put in a good thick Piece of Bread, some Whole Pepper, a Blade or two of Mace; boil it five or six Minutes till the Bread is soft, then take out all the Spice and pour out all the Water, only just enough to keep it moist, beat it with a Spoon soft, throw in a little Salt, and a good Piece of fresh Butter; stir it well together, set it over the fire for a Minute or two, then put it into a Boat.

Surbiton, Kingston, 1751

To Roast Pheasants

If you have but one Pheasant, take a large fine Fowl about the Bigness of a Pheasant, pick it nicely with the Head on, draw it and truss it with the head turn'd as you do Pheasant's, lard the Fowl all over the Breast and Legs with a large Piece of Bacon cut in little Pieces; when roasted put them both in a Dish, and no Body will know it. They will take an Hour doing, as the Fire must not be too brisk. A *Frenchman* would order Fish Sauce to them, but then you quite spoil your Pheasants.

Surbiton, Kingston, 1751

28

To Boil Pigeons

BOIL them by themselves, for fifteen Minutes, then boil a handsome square Piece of Bacon and lay in the Middle; stew some Spinach to lay round, and lay the Pigeons on the Spinach. Garnish your Dish with Parsley laid in a Plate before the Fire to crisp. Or you may lay one Pigeon in th Middle, and the rest round, and the Spinach between each Pigeon, and a Slice of Bacon on each Pidgeon. Garnish with Slices of Bacon and melted Butter in a Cup.

Surbiton, Kingston, 1751

To Roast Pigeons

FILL them with Parsley clean wash'd and chopp'd, and some Pepper and Salt rolled in Butter; fill the Bellies, tye the Neck-end close, so that nothing can run out, put a Skewer through the Legs, and have a little Iron on purpose, with six Hooks to it, and on each Hook hang a Pigeon; fasten one End of the String to the Chimney, and the other End to the Iron (this is what we call the poor Man's Spit) flour them, baste them with Butter, and turn them gently for fear of hitting the Bars. They will roast nicely and be full of Gravy. Take Care how you take them off, not to lose any of the Liquor. You may melt a very little Butter, and put into the Dish. Your Pigeons ought to be quite Fresh, and not too much done. This is by much the best Way of doing them, for then they will swim in their own Gravy, and a very little melted Butter will do.

When you roast them on a Spit all the Gravy runs out, or if you stuff them and broil them Whole you cannot save the Gravy so well, though they will be very good with Parsley and Butter in the Dish, or split and broiled with Pepper and Salt.

Surbiton, Kingston, 1751

Pigeons transmogrified *

TAKE your Pigeons, season them with Pepper and Salt, take a large Piece of Butter, make a Puff-paste, and roll each Pigeon in a Piece of Paste; tie them in a Cloth, so that the Paste don't break; boil them in a good deal of Water. They will take an Hour and a Half boiling; untie them carefully that they don't break; lay them in the Dish, and you may pour a little good Gravy in the Dish. They will eat exceeding good and nice, and will yield Sauce enough of a very agreeable Relish.

Surbiton, Kingston, 1751

To pot Pigeons or fresh Fowl

FOR 2 persons take 4 large wood pigeons, parsley, 1 tablespoon mixed fresh herbs, a little nutmeg, salt pepper, ½ to ³/₄ lb butter. Put pigeons into earthenware dish, dab birds with butter and surround with remainder of butter, cook with gentle heat until tender - remove bones, return to pot, and heat until covers all flesh to keep weeks.

Weybridge, 17th. Century

* transmogrify = change the appearance of (*Oxford English Dictionary*)

PRESERVING MEAT

Cobbett's Receipt for Curing Bacon

RUB inside of the flitches (the two sides) with salt, place one on the other, flesh side uppermost, in the salting trough that has a drain. To have sweet fine bacon, change the salt once in four or five days, and change the flitches putting the bottom one on top a couple of times, this will cost more in salt but keep better. The time required to make the flitches sufficiently salt, will depend on thickness, weather, and where salting is taking place. Flitches of a hog of five score about six weeks will do it depending on the weather, if fat it will not come to harm by over salting and keep to Christmas. Salting should take place in a room with a good breeze blowing through, similar to a dairy to avoid tainting the meat. To smoke, two precautions are necessary first hang 'where no rain comes down', and smoke with wood, not peat turf or coal, smoke, the time taken depends on whether the fire is constant, large or small, if constant a month, but too long hanging in the air makes the bacon rust. The flitch must be perfectly dry but not as dry as a board. Before hanging up, lay it on the floor, seal the flesh side thickly with bran or sawdust, but not of deal or fir, and pat down for to form a crust to dry on.

To keep put fine clean wood ash in a box, lay in one flitch, cover with ash, lay in the second flitch and cover with six or eight inches of ash - with these precautions the bacon will be as good a year on.

Abridged from *Cottage Economy*, 1823

Brine for Beef

1 lb of Bay salt to six quarts of water 1 oz of salt petre one oz of coarse moist sugar, two handfuls of coarse salt, boil it half an hour and when cold it is fit for use.

Roundhurst, Haslemere, 19th. Century

Brine for Hams

3 lbs of coarse salt, 2oz of saltpetre and one pint of treacle to 2 gallons of water, the hams to be turned every day and to be kept down under the pickle with a brick.

Roundhurst, Haslemere, 19th. Century

To make Mutton Hams

YOU must take a Hind-Quarter of Mutton, cut it like a Ham, take one Ounce of Salt-petre, a Pound of coarse Sugar, a Pound of common Salt; mix them and rub your Ham, lay it in a hollow Tray with the Skin downwards, baste it every Day for a Fortnight, then roll it in Sawdust, and hang it in the Wood-smoke a Fortnight; then boil it, and hang it in a dry Place, and cut it out in Rashers. It don't eat well boiled, but eats finely broiled.

Surbiton, Kingston, 1751

To pickle Pork

BONE your Pork, cut it into Pieces, of a Size fit to lye in the Tub or Pan you design it to lye in, rub your Pieces well with Salt-petre, then take two Parts of common Salt and two of Bay-salt, and rub every Piece well; lay a Layer of common Salt in the Bottom of your Vessel, cover every Piece over with common Salt, lay them one upon another as close as you can, filling the hollow Places on the Sides with Salt. As your Salt melts on the Top, strew on more, lay a coarse Cloth over the Vessel, a Board over that, and a Weight on the Board to keep it down. Keep it close covered; it will thus ordered keep the whole year. Put a Pound of Salt-petre, and two Pounds of Bay-salt to a Hog.

Surbiton, Kingston, 1751

To dry a Goose

GET a fat Goose, take a Handful of common Salt, a Quarter of an Ounce of Salt-Petre, a Quarter of a Pound of coarse Sugar, mix all together, and rub your Goose very well, let it lie in this Pickle a Fortnight, turning and rubbing it every Day, then roll it in Bran, and hang it up in a Chimney where wood-Smoke is for a Week. If you have not that Conveniency send it to the Bakers, the Smoke of the Oven will dry it; or you may hang it in your own Chimney, not too near the Fire, but make a Fire under it, and lay Horse-Dung and Saw-Dust on it, and that will smother and smoke-dry it; when it is well dried keep it in a dry Place, you may keep it two or three Months or more; when you boil it put in a good deal of Water, and be sure to skim it well.

Surbiton, Kingston, 1751

To pot a Cold Tongue, Beef, or Venison

CUT it small, beat it well in a Marble Mortar, with melted Butter, and two Anchovies, till the Meat is mellow and fine; then put it down close in your Pots, and cover it with clarified Butter. Thus you may do cold Wild Fowl; or you may pot any Sort of cold Fowl whole seasoning them with what Spice you please.

Surbiton, Kingston, 1751

MADE DISHES

Rules to be Observed in all Made Dishes

FIRST, that the Stew-pans, or Sauce-pans and Covers be very clean, free from Sand and well tinn'd; and that all the White Sauces have a little Tartness, and be very smooth and of a fine Thickness, and all the Time any White Sauce is over the Fire keep stirring it one Way.

Surbiton, Kingston, 1751

To make a White Fricasey

YOU may take two Chickens or Rabbits, skin them and cut them into little Pieces. Lay them into warm water to draw out all the Blood, and then lay them in a clean Cloth to dry: Put them in a Stew-pan with Milk and Water, stew them till they are tender, and then take a clean Pan, put in Half a Pint of Cream and a Quarter of a Pound of Butter; stir it together till the butter is melted, but you must be sure to keep it stirring all the Time or it will be Greasy, and then with a Fork take the Chickens or Rabbits out of the Stew-pan and put into the Sauce-pan to the Butter and Cream. Have ready a little Mace dry'd and beat fine, a very little Nutmeg, a few Mushrooms, shake all together for a Minute or two, and dish it up. If you have no Mushrooms a Spoonful of the Pickle does full as well and gives it a pretty Tartness. This is a very pretty Sauce for a Breast of Veal roasted.

Surbiton, Kingston, 1751

To make Mock Goose

2lbs of breast of mutton, bone & spread flat, 5 slices of bread soak and squeeze dry, cut up one onion & mix with chopped sage, one beaten egg, salt & pepper, spread mixture on meat, roll up in a cloth & simmer for 1½ hours, or roast in front of fire until brown.

Rowtown, Chertsey, 19th. Century

To make Common Sausages

TAKE three Pounds of nice Pork, Fat and Lean together, without Skin or Gristles; chop it as fine as possible, season it with a Tea Spoonful of beaten Pepper, and two of Salt, some Sage shred fine, about three Tea Spoonfuls; mix it well together, have the Guts very nicely cleaned, and fill them, or put them down in a Pot, so roll them of what Size you please, and fry them. Beef makes very good Sausages.

Surbiton, Kingston, 1751

Rules to be observed in making boiled Puddings &c.

IN boiled Puddings, take great Care the Bag or Cloth be very clean, and not soapy, and dipped in hot Water, and then well floured. If a Bread-pudding, tie it loose; if a Batter-pudding, tie it close, and be sure the Water boils when you put the Pudding in, and you should move your Puddings in the Pot now and then, for fear they stick. When you make a Batter-pudding, first mix the Flour well with a little Milk, then put in the Ingredients by Degrees, and it will be smooth and not have Lumps; but for a plainBatter-pudding, the best Way is to strain it through a coarse Hair Sieve, that it may neither have Lumps, nor the Treadles of the Eggs: And all other Puddings, strain the Eggs when they are beat. If you boil them in Wooden Bowls, or China Dishes, butter the Inside before you put in your Batter; and all baked Puddings, butter the Pan or Dish, before the Pudding is put in.

Surbiton, Kingston, 1751

Sewet Dumplings

TAKE a Pint of Milk, four Eggs, a Pound of Sewet, and a Pound of Currants, two Tea Spoonfuls of Salt, three of Ginger; first take Half the Milk, and mix it like a thick Batter, then put the Eggs, and the Salt and Ginger, then the rest of the Milk by Degrees, with the Sewet and Currants, and Flour to make it like a light Paste. When the Water boils, make them in Rolls as big as a large Turkey's Egg, with a little Flour; then flat them, and throw them into boiling Water. Move them softly, that they don't stick together, keep the Water boiling all the Time, and Half an Hour will boil them.

Surbiton, Kingston, 1751

Hogs Pudding

1 Gallon of flour, strike measure, and some bread, 1½lbs currants, sugar & spice as you please, boil them 3/4 of an hour.

Roundhurst, Haslemere, 19th. Century

A Steak Pudding

MAKE a good Crust, with Sewet shred fine with Flour, and mix it up with cold Water. Season it with a little Salt, and make a pretty stiff Crust, about two Pounds Sewet to a Quarter of a Peck of Flour. Let your Steaks be either Beef or Mutton, well season'd with Pepper and Salt, make it up as you do an Apple-pudding, tie it in a Cloth, and put it into the Water boiling. If it be a large Pudding, it will take five Hours; if a small one, three Hours. This is the best Crust for an Apple-pudding. Pigeons eat well this Way.

Surbiton, Kingston, 1751

33

Puff Paste

TAKE a Quarter of a Peck of Flour, rub fine Half a Pound of Butter, a little Salt, make it up into a light Paste with coldWater, just stiff enough to work it well up; then roll it out, and stick Pieces of Butter all over, and strew a little Flour; roll it up, and roll it out again; and so do nine or ten Times, till you have rolled in a Pound and Half of Butter. This Crust is mostly used for all Sorts of Pies.

Surbiton, Kingston, 1751

A Standing Crust for Great Pies

TAKE a Peck of Flourk and six Pounds of Butter, boiled in a Gallon of Water, skim it off into the flour, and as little of the Liquor as you can; work it well up into a Paste, then pull it into Pieces till it is cold, then make it up in what Form you will have it. This is fit for the Walls of a Goose Pye.

Surbiton, Kingston, 1751

A Beef Steak Pye

TAKE fine Rump Steaks, beat them with Rolling-pin, then season them with Pepper and Salt, according to your Palate. Make a good Crust, lay in your Steaks, fill your Dish, then pour in as much Water as will Half fill the Dish. Put on the Crust, and bake it well.

Surbiton, Kingston, 1751

A Bone Pie (Thursday night's supper !)

AFTER removing the meat from the bones for other dishes the bones must be slowly cooked for long time over gentle heat in well seasoned water, then placed in a pie dish with the liquid, which will become a thick jelly, Cover with pastry and bake.

Row Town, Chertsey, 19th. Century

To Season an Egg Pye

BOIL twelve Eggs hard, and shred them with one Pound of Beef Sewet, or Marrow shred fine. Season them with a little Cinnamon and Nutmeg beat fine, one Pound of Currants clean washed and picked, two or three Spoonfuls of Cream, and a little Sack and Rose Water mixt all together, and fill the Pye. When it is baked, stir in Half a Pound of fresh Butter, and the Juice of a Lemon.

Surbiton, Kingston, 1751

To Make a Mutton Pye

TAKE a Loin of Mutton, take off the Skin and Fat of the Inside, cut it into Steaks; season it well with Pepper and Salt to your Palate. Lay it into your Crust, fill it pour in as much Water as will almost fill the Dish; then put on the Crust, and bake it well.

Surbiton, Kingston, 1751

VEGETABLES

IN THE MEDIEVAL period diners were advised not to eat fruit or vegetables particularly if raw.

To dress Greens, Roots, &c.

ALWAYS be very careful that your Greens be nicely picked and washed. You should lay them in a clean Pan for fear of Sand or Dust, which is apt to hang round wooden Vessels. Boil all your Greens in a Copper Sauce-pan by themselves, with a great Quantity of Water. Boil no Meat with them, for that discolours them. Use no Iron Pans, &c. for they are not proper; but let them be Copper, Brass or Silver.

Surbiton, Kingston, 1751

Directions concerning Garden Things

MOST People spoil Garden Things by over boiling them. All Things that are Green should have a little Crispness, for if they are over boil'd they neither have any Sweetness or Beauty.

Surbiton, Kingston, 1751

An amulet* of Beans

BLANCH your Beans, and fry them in sweet butter, with a little Parsley, pour out the Butter, and pour in some Cream. Let it simmer, shaking your Pan; season with Pepper, Salt and Nutmeg, thicken with three or four Yolks of Eggs, have ready a Pint of Cream, thickned with the Yolks of four Eggs, season with a little Salt, pour it in your Dish, and lay your Beans on the Amulet, and serve it up hot.

The same Way you may dress Mushrooms, Truffles, Green Peas, Asparagus, and Artichoke-bottoms, Spinach, Sorrel, &c. all being first cut into small Pieces, or shred fine.

Surbiton, Kingston, 1751

Brockely in Sallad

BROCKELY is a pretty Dish by way of Sallad in the Middle of a Table. Boil it like Asparagrus, lay it on your Dish, beat up Oil and Vinegar, and a little Salt. Garnish with Stertion-buds.§

Oxshott, 19th. Century

*　Amulet *probably* should be omelette.

§　Stertion-buds = Nastertium Seeds.

35

UTENSILS FOR FRUIT AND VEGETABLE PREPARATION

KEY (ITEMS ARE LISTED FROM LEFT TO RIGHT):-

1 **Early nineteenth-century, five-tier Spice Box.** Round boxes of all types were a speciality of Sussex.

2 **A Pear-shaped Chopping Board with attached Knife.** The straight sides denote a Victorian date.

3 **Pie Peel,** with six-inch blade. Peels for bread had eight-to-ten-inch blades.

4 **Bone Wheel Cutter.**

5 **Nineteenth-century Acorn Nutmeg Grater.**

6 **Hair Sieve.** 'Shaker' sieves were probably based on this type.

7 **Hurt Picker,** for picking whortleberries, known in Surrey as 'hurts', a name which lingers in some place names, e.g. Hurt Hill, Hurt Common.

8 **Pewter Pepper Pot or Muffineer.**

9 **A nineteenth-century Lemon Squeezer,** with pottery strainer.

To dress Carrots

LET them be scraped very clean, and when they are enough rub them in a clean Cloth, then slice them into a Plate, and pour some melted Butter over them. If they are young Spring Carrots, Half an Hour will boil them; if large, an Hour; but old Sandwich Carrots will take two Hours.

Surbiton, Kingston, 1751

To fry Cauliflower

TAKE two fine cauliflowers, boil them in milk and water, then leave one whole, pull the other to pieces; take half a pound of butter with two spoonfuls of water, a little dust of flour, and melt the butter in a stew-pan, then put in the whole cauliflower cut in two, the other pulled to pieces and fry it until it is of a very light brown. Season with pepper and salt. When it is enough lay the two halves in the middle and pour the rest all over it.

Dormansland, 19th. Century

Celery Sauce

THE Celery must be boil'd quite tender, then Put it into Some Strong Broth, made with Veal and Ham, Let it Stew a Little, then Thicken it with Butter and Flour, and Bind it with the Yolks of two Eggs and a Little Cream well Beaten together; and then put in the Juice of half a Lemon, But be sure not to Let it Boil after the Eggs and Cream are in. Good Sauce for Boil'd Fowls.

Worplesdon, 1779

To Ragoo Cucumbers

TAKE two Cucumbers, two Onions, slice them and fry them in a little Butter; then drain them in a Sieve, put them into a Sauce-pan, add six spoonfuls of Gravy, two of White Wine, a Blade of Mace: Let them stew five or six Minutes; then take a Piece of Butter as big as a Walnut rolled in Flour, shake them together, and when it is thick dish them up.

Surbiton, Kingston, 1751

A Fricasey of Kidney Beans

TAKE a Quart of the Seed, when dry, soak them all Night in River Water, then boil them on a slow Fire till quite tender; take a Quarter of a Peck of Onions, slice them thin, fry them in Butter till Brown; then take them out of the Butter, and put them in a Quart of strong draw'd Gravy. Boil them till you may mash them fine, then put in your Beans, and give them a boil or two. Season with Pepper, Salt, and Nutmeg.

Surbiton, Kingston, 1751

Stewed Peas and Lettuce

TAKE a Quart of Green Peas, two nice Lettuce clean washed and picked, cut them small across, put all into a Sauce-pan with a Quarter of a Pound of Butter, Pepper and Salt to your Palate; cover them close, and let them stew softly, shaking the Pan often. Let them stew ten Minutes, then shake in a little Flour, toss them round, and pour in Half a Pint of good Gravy; put in a little Bundle of Sweet Herbs and an Onion, with three cloves, and a Blade of Mace stuck in it. Cover it close, and let them stew a Quarter of an Hour; then take out the Onion and Sweet Herbs, and turn it all into a Dish. If you find the Sauce not thick enough, shake in a little more Flour, and let it simmer, then take it up.

Surbiton, Kingston, 1751

To make Potatoe Cakes

TAKE Potatoes, boil them, peel them, beat them in a Mortar, mix them with Yolks of Eggs, a little Sack. Sugar, a little beaten Mace, a little Nutmeg, a little Cream or melted Butter, work it up into a Paste; then make it into Cakes, or just what Shapes you please with Molds, fry them Brown in fresh Butter, lay them in Plates or Dishes, melt Butter with Sack and Sugar, and pour over them.

Surbiton, Kingston, 1751

A Pudding made thus

MIX it as before, make it up in the Shape of a Pudding, and bake it; pour Butter, Sack and Sugar over it.

Surbiton, Kingston, 1751

Stewed Red Cabbage

TAKE a Red Cabbage, lay it in cold Water an Hour, then cut it into thin Slices across, and cut it into little Pieces. Put it into a Stew-pan, with a Pound of Sausages, a Pint of Gravy, a little bit of Ham or lean Bacon; cover it close, and let it stew Half an Hour; then take the Pan off the Fire, and skim off the Fat, shake in a little Flour, and set it on again. Let it stew two or three Minutes, then lay the Sausages in your Dish, and pour the rest all over. You may, before you take it up, put in Half a Spoonful of Vinegar.

Surbiton, Kingston, 1751

How to cook Salsify*

WASH it well but do not scrape it, throw into boiling salted water; and when tender take it out and peel. Eat with a good sauce.

Weybridge, late 18th. Century

*   Salsify, an indiginous root vegetable.

To boil Spinach, when you have not Room on the Fire, to do by itself

HAVE a Tin-box, or any other Thing that shuts very close, put in your Spinach, cover it so close as no Water canget in, and put it into Water or a Pot of Liquor, or any Thing you are boiling. It will take about an Hour, if the Pot or Copper boils. In the same Manner you may boil Peas without Water.

Surbiton, Kingston, 1751

To make a Spinach Pudding

TAKE a Quarter of a Peck of Spinach, picked and washed clean, put it into a Sauce-pan, with a little Salt, cover it close, and when it is boiled just tender, throw it into a Sieve to drain; then chop it with a Knife, beat up six Eggs, mix well with it Half a Pint of Cream and a stale Roll grated fine, a little Nutmeg, and a Quarter of a Pound of melted Butter; stir all well together, put it into the Sauce-pan you boiled the Spinach, and keep stirring it all the Time till it begins to thicken; then wet and flour your Cloth very well, tie it up and boil it an Hour. When it is enough, turn it into your Dish, pour melted Butter over it, and the Juice of a *Seville* Orange, if you like it; as to Sugar, you must add, or let it alone, just to your Taste. You may bake it; but then you should put in a Quarter of a Pound of Sugar. You may add Biscuit in the room of Bread, if you like it better.

Surbiton, Kingston, 1751

To fricasey Skirrets*

WASH the Roots very well, and boile them till they are tender; then the Skin of the Roots must be taken off, cut in Slices, and have ready a little Cream, a Piece of Butter rolled in Flour, the Yolk of an Egg beat, a little Nutmeg grated, two or three Spoonfuls of White Wine, a very little Salt, and stir all together. Your Roots being in the Dish, pour the Sauce over them. It is a pretty Side-dish. So likewise you may dress Root of Salsify and Scorzonera§.

Surbiton, Kingston, 1751

To raise a Sallad in two Hours at the Fire

TAKE fresh Horse-Dung hot, lay it in a Tub near the Fire, then sprinkle some Mustard-seeds thick on it, lay a thin Layer of Horse-Dung over it, cover it close and keep it by the Fire, and it will rise high enough to cut in two Hours.

Surbiton, Kingston, 1751

*   Skirret, or water parsnip, a root vegetable, formerly much grown in England.

§   Scorzonera, a root vegetable imported from Spain, somewhat like a Parsnip.

TARTS PUDDINGS & SWEETS

To make different Sorts of Tarts

IF you bake in Tin-patties, butter them, and you must put a little Crust all over, because of the taking them out; if in China, or Glass, no Crust but the Top one. Lay fine Sugar at the Bottom, then your Plumbs, Cherries, or any other Sort of Fruit, and Sugar at Top; then put on your Lid, and bake them in a slack Oven. Mince Pies must be baked in Tin-patties, because of taking them out, and Puff-paste is best for them. All sweet Tarts the beaten Crust is best; but as you Fancy. Apple, Pear, Apricot, &c. make thus; Apples and Pears, pare them, cut them into Quarters, and core them; cut the Quarters across again, set them on a Sauce-pan with just as much Water as will barely cover them, let them simmer on a slow Fire just till the Fruit is tender; put a good Piece of Lemon-peel in the Water with the Fruit, then have your Patties ready. Lay fine Sugar at Bottom, then your Fruit, and a little Sugar at Top; that you must put in at your Discretion. Pour over each Tart a Tea Spoonful of Lemon-Juice, and three Tea Spoonfuls of the Liquor they were boiled in; put on your Lid, and bake them in a slack Oven. Apricots do the same Way, only don't use Lemon.

If the Tart is not eat your Sweet Meat is not the worse and it looks genteel.

Surbiton, Kingston, 1751

Paste for Tarts

ONE Pound of Flour, three Quarters of a Pound of Butter; mix up together, and beat well with a Rolling-pin.

Surbiton, Kingston, 1751

To make Kickshaws

MAKE Puff-paste, roll it thin, and if you have any Moulds work it upon them, make them up with preserved Pippins. You may fill some with Gooseberries, some with Raspberries, or what you please, then close them up, and either bake or fry them; throw grated Sugar over them, and serve them up.

Surbiton, Kingston, 1751

Orange Tarts

TAKE two oranges, grate the peel with the juice of them and one lemon, ½ a pound of sugar, ¼ of a pd of fresh Butter, melted very carefully, 4 eggs leaving out 2 of the whites, beat them well together. A quarter hour will bake them. The patty pans must be lined with the rich crust. This quantity makes two dozen tarts.

Losely MS., Guildford, 17th. to 19th. Centuries.

(1379/121/160)

Maid of Honour Tarts

8 oz. puff pastry	2 teaspoons brandy
1 pt. fresh milk	½ oz. sweet almonds
1 teaspoon rennet	a little sugar
pinch of salt	a little ground cinnamon
4 oz. butter	rind and juice of ½ lemon
2 egg yolks	currants to decorate

Make the pastry. Warm the milk to blood heat, add the rennet and the salt. When the curds have set drain through a fine muslin, overnight. Rub the curds through a sieve with the butter. Beat the yolks of eggs to a froth with the brandy. Add to the curds. Blanch and chop the almonds and add them to the curds with a little sugar and cinnamon. Add the rind and juice of the lemon. Line the patty tins with puff pastry. Fill them with the mixture and sprinkle with currants. Bake in a medium to hot oven for 20 - 25 minutes, until risen and brown.

Hampton Court and Richmond Palace, 16th. Century

Great Granny Crisfield's Mincemeat

½ lb Prunes, cooked & chopped up	½ lb Seedless Raisins
³/₄ lb Currants	½ lb Apples chopped
½ lb Saltanas	½ lb Suet shredded
³/₄ lb Brown Sugar	¼ lb Mixed peel
1 Lemon juice & rind	½ pint Brandy
½ Nutmeg grated	½ teaspoon Ginger
½ teaspoon Mace	Salt

Mix all together and pack in jars.

Kingston, 19th. Century

Batter Pudding

TWO spoonsfull of flour mixed by degrees in a pint of cold milk, put it on the fire stir till it boils, put it out to cool, add a little salt and sugar, and 3 eggs, bake in an oven.

Roundhurst, Haslemere, 19th. Century

To mak Cheese Cake

TAKE 3 quarts of Milk and Straining itt through a Sive y^u work half a pound of butter through a Sive y^u put the yolks of 6 eggs in itt.

Farnham, 18th. Century

Good Friday Pudding

THIS is made with warm oatmeal mixt with eggs, milk, suet and penny-royal, boyle first in a linnen bag, and then stript and buttered with sweet butter.

Surrey, 1615

41

Farnham Pudding

3oz. Flour, half pint Milk, 3oz. Butter, 2oz. Loaf Sugar, 4 Eggs, 1 Teaspoon Essence Vanilla, ½ oz. chopped Candied Peel, mix the flour & milk perfectly smooth, add the butter & sugar & the slo boiling, add the Yolks each one separately beaten well, add the Vanilla. Whip thick the whites, mix well into Pudding, Butter a Mould, stick the peel to the bottom & sides; pour in mixed Pudding, a buttered paper on top, tie it up tight, put in a pan of boiling water to the middle of the mould, boil once, put it off the fire & simmer it for hour & half. Sauce rich milk with an egg beaten up in it and a glass of wine heated, not boiled.

Farnham, 1875

To make a Grateful Pudding

TAKE a Pound of fine Flour and a Pound of White Bread grated, take eight Eggs, but Half the Whites, beat them up, and mix with them a Pint of new Milk, then stir in the Bread and Flour, a Pound of Raisins stoned, a Pound of Currants, Half a Pound of Sugar, a little beaten Ginger; mix all well together, and either bake or boil it. It will take three Quarters of an Hour's baking. Put Cream in, instead of Milk, if you have it. It will be an Addition to the Pudding.

Surbiton, Kingston, 1751

Great Granny Crisfield's Christmas Pudding

1 lb Suet	1 lb Breadcrumbs
1 lb Dark brown sugar	¼ lb Flour
½ lb Valencia seedless raisons	1¼ lb Currants
½ lb Muscatel seedless raisons	¼ lb Candied peel
Rind of lemon (grated)	1½ Nutmegs (grated)
½ oz Ground cinnamon	¼ lb Saltanas
1 oz Bitter almonds (chopped)	¼ pt Brandy
4 Eggs	

Mix together and steam for 6 hours. (2 large & 1 small pudding).

Kingston, 19th. Century

Lemon Pudding

½ lb. Bread Crumbs, 6 oz. Suet, ½lb. Lump Sugar, 2 Eggs, 1 Lemon, boil it 1¾ hours.

Roundhurst, Haslemere, 19th. Century

To make Oatmeal Pudding

TAKE a porringer full of oatmeal beaten to flower a pint of cream one nuttmeg 4 Eggs beaten, a pound of sugar a pound of beef Suit Shrid small, mingle all together & y^u may bake itt in an our.

Farnham, 19th. Century

To make Potatoe Pudding

TAKE a Quart of Potatoes, boil them soft, peel them and mash them with a Back of a Spoon, and rub them through a Sieve, tohave them fine and smooth; take Half a Pound of fresh Butter melted, Half a Pound of fine Sugar, so beat them well together till they are very smooth, beat six Eggs, Whites and all, stir them in, and a Glass of Sack or Brandy. You may add Half a Pound of Currants, boil it Half an Hour, melt Butter with a Glass of White Wine; sweeten with Sugar, and pour over it. You may bake it in a Dish, with Puff-paste all round the Dish and at the Bottom.

Surbiton, Kingston, 1751

Surrey Frumenty

INTO a fireproof jar put cooked crushed wheat, sugar raisons and spice, as you please, cover with skimmed milk, and leave at the back of the fire all night, sweaten again & send to the table after the meat [also traditionally eaten at breakfast on Christmas morning].

Rowtown, Chertsey, 19th. Century

Apricot Cream

¼ pint Apricot Pulp	¼ pint Cream	2 Eggs
½ oz. Gelatine	¼ pint Milk	1 oz. Sugar

Separate the whites from the yolks of eggs. Rub the apricots through a sive, melt the gelatine in the milk, add the eggs and cream and sugar, last of all the whipped whites, put in a mold.

Shere, 1897

To make Bowe Mange

TAKE 3oz of Isinglass, & pour a kettle of boiling water upon it, let it stand all night, then pour the water from it, & put 3 pints of Cream, a handful of sweet almonds & a few Bitter Ditto to flavour beat it extremely fine, sweeten it to your taste boyle it up & Strain it through a Lawn Sive keep it Stirring till it is cool and let it settle a little before you put it into dishes.

Losely MS., Guildford, 17th. to 19th. Centuries. (1379/208)

To make boiled Custard

TAKE Milk & boyle wth a blade of Mace y^u take itt of & lett it Stand till almost Cold y^u beate y^r Eggs & Sugar very small & y^u simer it up.

Farnham, 19th. Century

Crystal Palace Pudding

½ oz. gelatine, 3/4 pt. milk, 2 teaspoonfuls cornflower, 2 oz. sugar, ½ teaspoonful vanilla, 2 egg yolks, a little angelica and glacé cherries.

Mix the cornflower with a little cold milk, boil remainder of milk and add to the mixture, cook for five minutes. Add the sugar, flavouring and the gelatine, dissolved in a little hot water. Place the pieces of angelica and cherries at the bottom of small dariol moulds and fill with the cornflour mixture. When cold, dip in hot water and turn out the puddings. Serve with cold raspberry sauce prepared by boiling 2 tablespoonfuls of raspberry jam, 1 tablespoonful sugar and ¼ pint of water for 10 minutes and then straining.

Croydon, 19th. Century

To make Fine Pancakes

TAKE Half a Pint of Cream, Half a Pint of Sack, the yolks of eighteen eggs beat fine, a little Salt, Half a Pound of fine Sugar, a little beaten Cinnamon, Mace, and Nutmeg; then put in as much Flour as will run thin over the Pan, and fry them in fresh Butter. This Sort of Pancake will not be crisp, but very good.

Surbiton, Kingston, 1751

To make Possets

TAKE a Pint of Cream, Boil it and let it Stand to be Cold, and the Night before you make them Peel a Lemon and let it stand all night in half a Pint of Mountain* Wine then Strain your Cream into a Pot then Sweeten your Wine. Put in the Juice of a Lemon, then mix it all together, take the froth as it rises, and put into glasses.

Worplesdon, 1779

Lord John Russell's Pudding

6 Eggs (yolks only)
1½ pints Milk
1 oz. Isinglass
1½ oz. loaf Sugar
½ pint Cream

1 wine glass Brandy
Ratafia essence
Preserved pineapple
Citron and orange peel
Cherries and any other dried fruit

Beat eggs with milk and put into a pan, add grated lemon peel, sugar and isinglass, whisk over a slow fire till isinglass dissolved, and mixture thickened, add cream, and then brandy and a little ratafia essence, cook and thicken but do not boil and then stir in the candied fruit, pour into a quart mould, cover. Put in an ice cave, or make sure it is sealed and stand in bucket of ice mixed with freezing salt, pack all round and cover with a blanket.

Ruxley Lodge, Esher, 1863

* Mountain is a variety of Malaga Wine

BUNS, ROLLS, BISCUITS & CAKES

Bread

Until at least the mid 1770s. an oven was mainly used for making 'flour-baked' food: bread, pies, cakes, &c. Lighted brushwood was put inside the oven and left until the oven was hot. The ashes were then raked out and the food put in to cook. It was put in and taken out with a *Peel*. Ovens have sometimes taken three days to reach the required heat.

Instructions for building ovens were as follows:

Note: In the building your Oven observe that you make it round, low roofed and a little Mouth; then it will take less Fire and keep the Heat better than a long Oven and high roofed, and will bake the Bread better.

Surbiton, Kingston, 1751

To make Breakfast Cakes

HALF a quarter of Flour, two spoonfuls of Yeast, a quarter of a Pound of Melted Butter in a Pint of Milk two Eggs, a Little Salt, mix all and Let it Stand all night, in the morning make it up into Cakes and Bake them.

Worplesdon, 1779

A Good Bunn

7 lbs Flour, 1lb Sugar, 2lbs Currants, 1lb Butter, spice & 2lbs of Peel.

Roundhurst, Haslemere, 19th. Century

Guildford Manchets*

Get 1 or 2 pounds of dough in the morning, then butter & lard as you use in puff pastry, and work similar. Be sure and sprinkle salt. Use dough the same morning, prove well before and after being on tin, keep out of draught, work through centre only. Before baking was over lightly brush with egg or milk.

Guildford, 19th. Century

---

* 'The best and finest kind of Bread is Manchet.' 1736, quoted in *Oxford English Dictionary*.

To make Light Wigs[§]

TAKE a Pound and a Half of Flour, and half a Pint of Milk made warm, mix these together, cover it up and let it lye by the fire Half an Hour; then take Half a Pound of Sugar, and Half a Pound of Butter, then work these into a Paste and make it into Wigs, with as little Flour as possible. Let the Oven be pretty quick, and they will rise very much. Mind to mix a Quarter of a Pint of good Ale Yeast in Milk.

Surbiton, Kingston, 1751

To make Common Biscuits

BEAT up six Eggs, with a Spoonful of Rose Water and a Spoonful of Sack, then add a Pound of fine powdered Sugar, and a Pound of Flour; mix them into the Eggs by Degrees, and an ounce of Coriander-seeds, mix all well together, shape then on white thin Paper, or Tin Moulds, in any Form you please. Beat the White of an Egg, with a Feather rub them over, and dust fine Sugar over them. Set them in an Oven moderately heated, till they rise and come to a good Colour, take them out and when you have done with the Oven, if you have no stove to dry them in, put them in the Oven again, and let them stand all Night to dry.

Surbiton, Kingston, 1751

Grandfather's Fruit Biscuits

SCALD 3 lbs. of ripe gooseberries; i.e. put them without any water into a jar and place this in a pan of boiling water and boil till quite soft. Add 3lbs. finely powdered loaf sugar, and the whites of 2 eggs, whisk all until stiff enough to hang in the whisk, drop in teaspoonfuls on to white paper and dry gradually by the fire; not too much heat or the colour will spoil.

Raspberries or black currants maÎ be also used with a little more sugar; also damsons. You may keep them in tin canisters for years. Difficult to succeed with, but very good.

West Clandon, 1840

Cold Water Willies*

Flour, salt and water, mixed to form a stiff dough & then into little cakes & baked hard.

Rowtown, Chertsey, 19th. Century

[§] "Home to the only Lenten supper I have had of Wiggs and Ale". Pepys.

* A plain hard biscuit used as bread in hard times and until 1900 in the Workhouse. They were often dunked in the liquid of anything that had been cooked, to make them more edible.

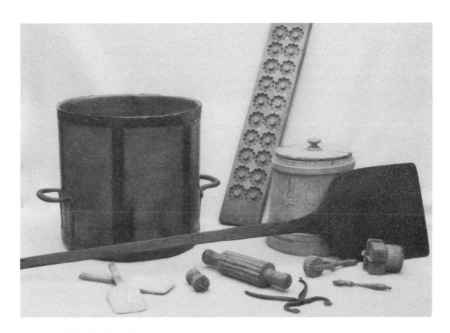

ITEMS IN USE IN BAKING

KEY (ITEMS ARE LISTED CLOCKWISE STARTING FROM 12 O'CLOCK):-

1   **Nineteenth-century Gingerbread or Biscuit Mould.** Gingerbread, often made from stale bread, was sold in Surrey markets until the middle of last century. Special moulds, such as Coats of Arms could be commissioned from carvers.

2   **Nineteenth-century Flour Bin,** the middle one of a set.

3   **Iron Bread Peel,** for removing hot faggots from the oven and for putting in and taking out the bread.

4   **Hot Cross Bun Marker,** with knob handle at back.

5   **Pastry marker or jigger.**

6   **Pastry Roller.**

7   **Sugar Snips**

8   **Roller or Crusher,** for oats, etc.

9   **Biscuit Pricker.**

10 **Butter Patters,** sometimes known as butter hands or butter boards. Butter making was summer work.

11 **Victorian Grain Measure,** banded with metal handles. All legal measures had to be marked with the quantity and the reign.

To make Little Fine Cakes

ONE pound of Butter beat to Cream, a Pound and a Quarter of Flour, a Pound of fine Sugar beat fine, a Pound of Currants clean washed and picked, six Eggs, two Whites left out, beat them fine, mix the Flour, Sugar and Eggs by Degrees into the Batter, beat it all well with both Hands, either make into little Cakes, or bake it in one.

Surbiton, Kingston, 1751

Hunting Gingerbread Nuts

3lbs Treacle, 1lb coarse raw sugar, 1lb butter, rubbed into 4lbs flour, ginger to taste & bake in a slow oven.

Roundhurst, Haslemere, 19th. Century

Guildford Royal Plum Cake

BY the late seventeenth century, it seems to have become the custom for the Corporation of Guildford to provide cakes when royalty visited the town. Two were baked in 1674, when the Duke of York (later James II) came. In 1957, the present Queen visited and a cake baked to the following recipe was presented to her:

Butter	1 lb.	Castor Sugar	8 oz.
Brown Sugar	8 oz.	Eggs	10
Flour	1 lb. 4 oz.	Ground Almonds	4 oz.
Currants	1 lb. 8 oz.	Cut Citron Peel	2 oz.
Sultanas	2 lb.	Cut Orange and Lemon Peel	2 oz.
Whole Cherries	8 oz.	Zest of 2 Oranges	
Mace	1/8 oz.	Cinnamon	1/8 oz.
Brandy	1 oz.	Sherry	1 oz.

The butter and sugar were creamed light and the eggs gradually added. The fruit was then well mixed in (the brandy and sherry having previously been poured on to the fruit) and the flour and ground almonds lightly mixed in. 7½ lb. of this mixing was then weighed into a 10 inch round hoop and baked for 4½ hours at a temperature of 330 ° F.

Guildford Museum

Nutmeg Cake

RUB three quarters of a Pound of Butter and a quarter of a Pound of Sugar into two Pounds of Flour, add a pennyworth of Yeast and half a pint of Lukewarm Milk with two Eggs and a large Nutmeg ground. Put before the fire until it rises up & let it be buttered, & be careful not to have it wetted.

Losely MS., Guildford, 17th. to 19th. Centuries. (1379/112)

To make Seed Cake

TAKE a pound of flower and 3qrs of a pound Caraway Seeds & some Sugar, a little Currant & Seed beate very fine, half a pint of Creame, a little Spice, half a pint of Butter milked, half a pint of Ale 2 whites and 4 yolks or 4 Eggs mixed all together very well, bake itt an our.

Farnham, 19th. Century

Soda Cake

½ lb Butter rubbed in a pound of flour, ½ lb of loaf sugar rolled, ½lb currants, mix three eggs with ¼ pint milk warmed, beat it well, the last thing put a small teaspoonful of soda, heat it a few minutes more, and put it in the oven as soon as possible. N.B. Good moist sugar with 6 ozs of butter is quite enough.

Roundhurst, Haslemere, 19th. Century

Sponge Cake

AS much lump sugar as the weight of six eggs, as much flour as the weight of 4 eggs, beat the white and yolks separately, put the sugar to the yolks, beat it up, then pour the whites on it, dry the flour, let it get quite cold, and about half an hour before you put it in the oven, mix it well with the eggs, fill the moulds about half full.

Roundhurst, Haslemere, 19th. Century

THE SURREY BRICK OVEN, exterior and interior views from Gertrude Jekyll, *Old English Household Life*, 1925.

EGGS & DAIRY PRODUCE

To make an Egg as big as Twenty

PART the Yolks from the Whites, strain them both separate through a Sieve, tye the Yolks up in a Bladder in the Form of a Ball. Boil them hard, then put this Ball into another Bladder, and the Whites round it; tye it up oval Fashion, and boil it. These are used for grand Sallads. This is very pretty for a Ragoo, boil five or six Yolks together, and lay in the Middle of the Ragoo of Eggs; and so you may make them of any Size you please.

Surbiton, Kingston, 1751

To broil Eggs

CUT a Toast round a Quartern Loaf, toast it Brown, lay it on your Dish, butter it, and very carefully break six or eight Eggs on the Toast, and take a red-hot Shovel, and hold over them. When they are done, squeeze a *Seville* Orange over them, grate a little Nutmeg over it, and serve it up for a Side-plate. Or you may poach your Eggs, and lay them on the Toast or toast your Toast crisp, and pour a little boiling Water over it; season it with a little Salt, and then lay your poached Eggs on it.

Surbiton, Kingston, 1751

To dress Eggs with Bread

TAKE a Penny-Loaf, soak it in a Quart of hot Milk for two Hours, or till the Bread is soft, then strain it through a coarse Sieve, put to it two Spoonfuls of Orange-flower Water, or Rose-Water; sweeten it, grate in a little Nutmeg, take a little Dish, butter the Bottom of it, break in as many eggs as will cover the Bottom of the Dish, pour in the Bread and Milk, set it in a Tin Oven before the Fire, and Half an Hour will bake it; or it will do on a Chaffing-dish of Coals. Cover it close before the Fire, or bake it in a slow Oven.

Surbiton, Kingston, 1751

Cheese Eggs

¼ lb cheese, minced parsley little, 6 eggs, butter pepper salt. Grate the cheese into a bakeing dish, mix seasoning, set it on stove & stir constantly, when cheese is melted, add egg previouly broken, still until they begin to get stiff.

Shere, 1897

IMPLEMENTS FROM THE DAIRY

KEY (ITEMS ARE LISTED CLOCKWISE STARTING FROM 12 O'CLOCK):-

1 **Stele** or whey bowl, a bowl with gauze covered central hole.

2 **Brig.** This is a frame which carries the Stele.

3 **A Sycamore Bowl** receives the whey drained through the gauze. Sycamore was chosen for use in kitchens and dairies because it does not flavour food.

4 **A Coopered Cheese Vat or Chessel, with its Follower or Sinker.** This specimen has five weep holes, but they can have up to eight. The follower is 1½ inches thick. This pair is in elm, but they are also made in sycamore.

5 **Cheese Print.** These can be very elaborately carved.

6 **A nineteenth-century Pottery 'Bowe Mange' Dish.**

7 **An eighteenth-century Chocolate Mill.** Mrs. Raffold advised making Syllabub with Chocolate in 1789.

8 **'Saucer' Cream Skimmer** in Sycamore.

9 **Butter Print.**

10 **Coopered Ice Bucket,** with small drainage hole at the base.

The dairy often had an Elder planted outside to keep the witches away, otherwise they might turn the milk sour or prevent the butter 'coming'. Although a long and widely held superstition, there are grounds today for thinking that Elders repel flies, which can affect milk and butter.

Eggoletts

3 Good Eggs (well beaten)	1 Onion (cut up small)
3 oz Flour	1 handful small Parsley chopped
6 oz Cheese (well shred)	Butter for frying, pepper & salt

While the butter heats in a pan over the fire, mix all the other ingredients, & drop small spoonfuls in the pan & fry.

Croydon, 19th. Century

A Fricasay of Eggs

BOIL eight Eggs hard, take off the shells, cut them into quarters, have ready Half a Pint of Cream, and a Quarter of a Pound of fresh Butter; stir it together over the Fire, till it is thick and smooth, lay the Eggs in your Dish, and pour the Sauce all over. Garnish with the hard Yolks of three Eggs cut into two and lay round the Edge of the Dish.

Surbiton, Kingston, 1751

To make an English Rabbit

TOAST a Slice of Bread Brown on both Sides, then lay it in a Plate before the Fire, pour a Glass of Red Wine over it, and let it soak the Wine up; then cut some cheese very thin, and lay it very thick over the Bread, put it in a Tin Oven before the Fire, and it will be toasted and brown'd presently. Serve it away hot.

Surbiton, Kingston, 1751

Hatted Kit

SKIM the curds from the whey & serve with blackberries & cream.

South Croydon, 19th. Century

Potted Cheese

BEAT a pound of strong cheese in a mortar, heat 2oz. butter and add to cheese, together with ½ glass of white wine, a pinch of cayenne and salt to taste, pot and seal with butter.

Chertsey, 19th. Century

PRESERVES

To keep Green Beans 12 Months

TAKE a wide mouth stone jar and cover the base with a layer of salt, then a layer of freshly prepared beans, then salt followed by beans, & repeat until jar is full, finish with a layer of salt, cover & have in a cool place. Care must be taken to replace cover as beans are removed, wash to remove excess salt & cook as with fresh beans.

South Croydon, 19th. Century

To keep Green Peas till Christmas

TAKE fine young Peas, shell them, throw them into boiling Water with some Salt in, let them boil five or six Minutes, throw them into a Cullender to drain, then lay a Cloth four or five Times double on a Table, and spread them on; dry them very well, and have your Bottles ready, fill them and cover them with Mutton-fat try'd; when it is a little cool fill the Necks almost to the Top, cork them, tie a Bladder and a Lath over them, and set them in a cool dry Place. When you use them boil your Water, put in a little Salt, some Sugar, and a Piece of Butter; when they are boiled enough, throw them into a Sieve to drain, then put them into a Sauce-pan with a good Piece of Butter, keep shaking it round all the Time till the Butter is melted, then turn them into a Dish, and send them to Table.

Surbiton, Kingston, 1751

To keep Mushrooms without Pickle

TAKE large Mushrooms, peel them, scrape out the Inside, put them into a Sauce-pan, throw a little Salt over them, and let them boil in their own Liquor; then throw them into a Sieve to drain, then lay them on Tin Plates, and set them in a cool Oven. Repeat it often till they are perfectly dry, put them into a clean Stone Jar, tie them down tight, and keep them in a dry Place. They eat deliciously, and look as well as Truffles.

Surbiton, Kingston, 1751

To preserve any Kind of Fruit

TO 6 lbs of fruit put 4 lbs sugar and after it begins to boil, let it boil 20 minutes, then put it in jars.

Roundhurst, Haslemere, 19th. Century

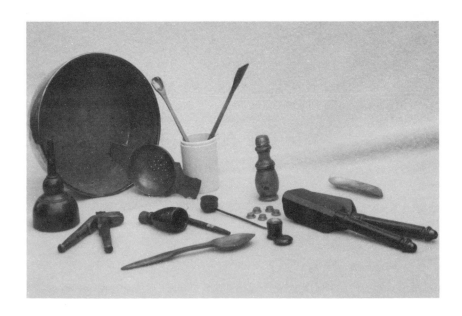

OBJECTS USED IN PRESERVING FOOD

KEY (ITEMS ARE LISTED FROM LEFT TO RIGHT):-

1 **Copper Preserving Pan.**

2 **Funnel.**

3 **Early nineteenth-century Nutcrackers,** with scrimshaw decoration on the head.

4 **Sycamore Strainer.**

5 **Horn Spoon.**

6 **Pestle and Mortar for Spice.**

7 **Nineteenth-century Stoneware Jam Jar.**

8 **Two Spoons** for sauce making.

9 **Small Ladle-shaped Measure,** believed to have been used for spice.

10 **Eighteenth-century Bottle Sealer with five Brass Signets,** each impressed with the name of a wine, and which fit onto a chuck in the hardwood handle.

11 **Pocket Nutmeg Grater.** The cap is decorated with a small piece of Tunbridge Ware.

12 **Seventeenth-century Lignum Vitae Lemon Squeezer,** held over a bowl to use, with the handles side-by-side.

13 **Horn Scoop or Measure.**

To Candy Cherries or Green Gages

DIP the Stalks and Leaves in White Wine Vinegar boiling, then scald them in Syrup; take them out and boil them to a candy Height; dip in the Cherries, and hang them to dry with the Cherries downwards. Dry them before the fire, or in the Sun. Then take the Plumbs, after boiling in the thin Syrup, peel off the Skin and candy them, and so hang them up to dry.

Surbiton, Kingston, 1751

Blackberry, Bilberry or Whortleberry Jelly

PICK the Fruit, bruise them slightly and put them into a Preserving-pan with just enough cold Water to cover them. Boil up and simmer until the Fruit is very soft. Put into a Jelly-bag (or a cloth suspended across two kitchen Chairs placed back to back) and let the Juice drip all night into a Pan placed under neath. Next day measure the Juice and weigh out one Pound of preserving Sugar to every Pint of Juice. Put into a Preserving-pan, and when Sugar is dissolved boil up quickly for about five Minutes or until it jellies when tested on a Plate.

Surbiton, Kingston, 1751

Medlar Jelly

TAKE Medlars when quite ripe and mash them, then put them into a preserving pan, with as much water as will just cover them, let them simmer very slowly till they become a pulp, the skins will break themselves, they must not be squeezed. Strain the juice through a jelly bag, letting it run of itself, and to every pint of juice put 3/4 lb. of the best loaf sugar. Boil it an hour and a half, taking off the scum as it rises, then put it into pots or moulds.

Suspend the jelly bag over basin on two chairs.

Roundhurst, Haslemere, 19th. Century

Quince Preserve*

PICK Quinces, halve & scoop out all core, put peel etc into saucepan & boil at least ½ hour then strain & put liquid over quince halves in covered oven dish & leave in cool oven four to six hours till quinces are soft, then take quinces out of liquid, arrange in jars, add sugar - 1 lb to 1 pint liquid & boil fast for 15 minutes, add syrup to quinces & seal quickly.

Dorking Town, 19th. Century

Preserving Rhubarb

7lbs rhubarb, 7lbs loaf sugar, 2 oz blanch almond, 2 lemons. Peel & cut rhubarb into pieces 1 inch long, put over gentle heat to extract juice. Add sugar warmed, grated peel and juice of lemons & sliced almonds, boil until thick & a deep colour 3/4 hr. app.

Addlestone, Chertsey, 1875

*   Quince Preserve was known in the eighteenth century as White Marmalade.

55

To preserve Strawberries in Wine

PUT a quantity of the finest large Strawberries into a gooseberry bottle and strew in 3 large spoons of fine sugar. Fill up with Madieira Wine or fine Sherry.

Chipstead, 19th. Century

To keep Walnuts all the Year

TAKE a large Jar, a Layer of Sea-sand at the Bottom, then a Layer of Walnuts, then Sand, then the Nuts, and so on till the Jar is full; and be sure they don't touch each other in any of the Layers. When you would use them, lay them in warm Water for an Hour, shifting the Water as it cools; then rub them dry, and they will peel well and eat sweet. Lemons will keep thus covered, better than any other Way.

Surbiton, Kingston, 1751

To candy any Sort of Flowers

TAKE the best treble-refined Sugar, break it into Lumps, and dip it Piece by Piece in Water, put them into a Vessel of Silver, and melt them over the Fire; when it just boils, strain it and let it on the Fire again, and let it boil till it draws in Hairs, which you may perceive by holding up your Spoon, then put in the Flowers, and set them in Cups or Glasses. When it is of a hard Candy, break it in Lumps, and lay it as high as you please. Dry it in a Stove, or in the Sun, and it will look like Sugar-candy.

Surbiton, Kingston, 1751

To Pickle Clove Gilly-Flowers for Sallads

TAKE the fairest Clove Gilly-Flowers, clip off the whites from them, put them into a Wide-mouthed Glass, and strew a good deal of sugar finely beaten among them, as will thoroughly Wet them, tye them up close and set them in the Sun, and in a little while they will be fit for use.

Worplesdon, 19th. Century

To make Syrup of Peach Blossoms

INFUSE Peach Blossoms in hot Water, as much as will handsomely cover them. Let them stand in Balneo, or in Sand, for twenty-four Hours covered close; then strain out the Flowers from the Liquor, and put in fresh Flowers. Let them stand to infuse as before, then strain them out, and to the Liquor put fresh Peach Blossoms the third Time; and, if you please, a fourth Time. Then to every Pound of your Infusion, add two Pounds of double-refined Sugar; and setting it in Sand, or Balneo, make a Syrup, which keep for Use.

Surbiton, Kingston, 1751

To make Conserve of Red Roses, or any other Flowers

TAKE Rose Buds, or any other Flowers, and pick them, cut off the white Part from the red, and put the red Flowers and sift them through a Sieve to take out the Seeds; then weigh them, and to every Pound of Flowers take two Pounds and a Half of Loaf Sugar; beat the Flowers pretty fine in a Stone Mortar, then by Degrees put the Sugar to them, and beat it very well till it is well incorporated together; then put it into Gallipots, tie it over with Paper, over that a Leather, and it will keep seven years.

Surbiton, Kingston, 1751

Crystallised Rose Petals

1½ cups of Red Rose Petals, ½ lb Castor Sugar, 1 eggwhite (beaten). Wash, drain & dry flower petals, add pink colouring to egg white, dip petals in egg & then sugar, dry on baking tray in slow oven, put in tin, keep apart with paper.

Haslemere Town, 19th. Century

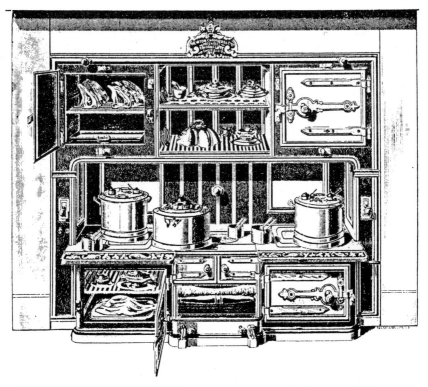

A CAST-IRON KITCHEN RANGE from a manufacturer's advertisement c.1880.

57

PICKLES, CHUTNEYS, &c

Rules to be observed in Pickling

ALWAYS use Stone Jars for all Sorts of Pickles, that require hot Pickle to them. The first Charge is the least, for these not only last longer, but keep the Pickle better; for Vinegar and Salt will penetrate through all earthen Vessels, Stone and Glass is the only Thing to keep Pickles in. Be sure never to put your Hands in to take Pickles out, it will soon spoil it. The best Way is, to every Pot tie a Wooden Spoon full of little Holes, to take the Pickles out with.

Surbiton, Kingston, 1751

Mixed Pickle

IN an earthenware pan a white cabbage sliced, 1 doz small onions in quarters, a cauliflower or cucumber cut in pieces, some French beans, 2 oz garlick, ½ pint shallots, some scraped horse-radish. Plentifully sprinkle with salt, & let them remain 3 days, then strain, shape neatly, & put them on a cloth in the sun to dry. Pack in jars and put near the fire. Boil the vinegar with pepper, cloves, mustard, chillies, ginger etc., & pour over boiling. Leave 2 months before eating.

Dorking Town, 19th. Century

Horse Radish Sauce

GRATE some horse radish very fine, add one tablespoonful of mustard, one of loaf sugar pounded very fine, ¼ pint thick cream, ¼ pint vinegar.

Roundhurst, Haslemere, 19th. Century

Apple or Plum Chutney

4 lbs apples - pealed etc. - or 4 lbs plums stoned, 1½ lbs moist sugar, 2 oz mustard seed, ½ lb chopped onions, 3 pts vinigar, 1 oz ground ginger, 1 oz ground allspice, a few capsicorms & chillies, pinch of salt. Boil all together for one hour or until reduced to pulp, remove from fire & add small teaspoonful of caen pepper. Ready for use or tie down.

Holmbury, 19th. Century

To pickle Artichoke-Bottoms

BOIL Artichokes till you can pull the Leaves off, then take off the Chokes, and cut them from the Stalk; take great Care you don't let the Knife touch the Top, throw them into Salt and Water for an Hour, then take them out and lay them on a Cloth to drain, then put them into large wide-mouthed Glasses, put a little Mace and sliced Nutmeg between, fill them either with distilled Vinegar, or your Sugar Vinegar and Spring-water; cover them with Mutton Fat try'd, and tie them down with a Bladder and Leather.

Surbiton, Kingston, 1751

To pickle Beans and Cucmbers

LET them lay in salt & water 24 hours, then put them in a cloth to dry, make a pickle of good vinegar ginger & pepper & put in a few grape leaves to boil in the vinegar, & some to put on top of the vegetables when they are in the jar, pour the pickle on boiling hot, cover close & set by the fire, continue boiling the vinegar every day, & putting fresh leaves in the jar until they are of a nice green colour.

Roundhurst, Haslemere, 19th. Century

An excellent Cattchup

AN excellent Cattchup M[rs]. Southall gave me for fish sauce, or any other sauce to put a little in. Take a quart of port Wine, half a handful of Horse Radish Roots cutt small, the same quantity of Parsley Roots cutt small, a quarter of a pound of Anchovies, as much black pepper pound'd fine, as will lye on half a Crown, let it Simmer all together over the fire, till it comes to a pint then strain it off - & bottle it, & cork it well for keeping, a little of this put into melted butter according to your own taste, makes exceeding good fish Sauce, you may warm it in the butter or not as you like - a little of this put in any other Sauce makes it very good.

Losely MS., Guildford, 17th. to 19th. Centuries. (1379/287)

Sweet Damson Pickle

2 lbs Damsons, 3/4 pt vinigar, 2 lbs loaf sugar, 1/4 teaspoonfuls cloves cinnamen. Prick damsons well all over, boil sugar & spice in vinigar & pour boiling over fruit, stand overnight, the strain off the liquor, & boil it again, next day bring all to boiling point & bottle.

Dorking Town, 19th. Century

Rhubarb Relish

1 quart Rhubarb, 1 quart onions, finely chopped, 1 pint vinegar, 1 tablespoonful Salt, 3 cupfuls of brown sugar, 1 teaspoonful each ginger, red pepper, cummin, allspice, black pepper. Boil all together until tender.

Dorking Town, 19th. Century

To burn Butter for thickening of Sauce

SET your Butter on the Fire, and let it boil till it is Brown, then shake in some Flour, and stir it all the Time it is on the Fire till it is thick. Put it bye, and keep it for Use. A little Piece is what the Cooks use to thicken and brown their Sauce; but there are few Stomachs it agrees with, therefore seldom make use of it.

Surbiton, Kingston, 1751

BEER AND WINE MAKING

KEY (ITEMS ARE LISTED FROM LEFT TO RIGHT):-

1 **Nineteenth-century Wooden Beaker Measure,** one of a set of three, each stamped 'V.R.' and with the quantity.

2 **Pewter Tankard,** also a measure and stamped similarly.

3 **Horn Beaker.**

4 **Large Stoneware Storage Bottle.**

5 **Two nineteenth-century Glass Toddy Stirrers.**

6 **Cellar Wine-bin Lable,** in white unglazed pottery.

7 **Eighteenth-century Corkscrew** (or 'steel worm'), with brush fitted to the handle.

8 **Nineteenth-century Glass Wine Bottle.**

9 **Spigot,** of mulberry wood.

10 **Oak Standing Cup.**

11 **A Nineteenth-century Coopered Costrel, Firkin or Keg.** Similar examples were issued to British troops before 1900.

12 **Late Nineteenth-century Stoneware Bottle** from Castle Brewery, Guildford.

ALE, GINGER BEER, & WINE

To make Ale

FOR 40 gallons put 15 pails of boiling water in the vat and two pails of cold, stirring it together, then put up 2 bushels of malt, mash it, and when the copper boils, the second time, let the beer run off and put 13 pails more of boiling water on the malt, then when the copper boils the third time, put up 27 pails for small beer, but that depends on the quantity required. Put the ale in the copper with 2lbs of hops, boil it one hour, then strain it and put the hops back into the copper with the small beer.

Roundhurst, Haslemere, 19th. Century

To make Birch Wine

THE Season for procuring the Liquor from the Birch Trees is in the Beginning of March, while the Sap is rising, and before the Leaves shoot out; for when the Sap is come forward, and the Leaves appear, the Juice by being long digested in the Bark, grows thick and colour'd, which before was thin and clear.

The Method of procuring the Juice is, by boring Holes in the Body of the Tree, and putting in Fossets, which are commonly made of the Branches of Elder, the Pith being taken out. You may without hurting the Tree, if large, tap it in several Places, four or five at a Time, and by that Means save from a good many Trees several Gallons every Day; if you have not enough in one Day, the Bottles in which it drops must be cork'd close, and rosined or waxed; however make use of it as soon as you can.

Take the Sap and boil it as long as any Scum rises, skimming it all the Time: To every Gallon of Liquor put four Pounds of good Sugar, the thin peel of a Lemon, boil it afterwards Half an Hour, scumming it very well, pour it into a clean Tub, and when it is almost cold, set it to work with Yeast spread on a Toast, let it stand five or six Days, stirring it often; then take such a Cask as will hold the Liquor, fire a large Match dipt in Brimstone, and throw it into the Cask, stop it close till the Match is extinguished, tun your Wine, lay the Bung on light till you find it has done working; stop it close and keep it three Months, then bottle it off.

Surbiton, Kingston, 1751

Dandelion Wine

GATHER the flowers on a fine dry day, measure them and put in a wooden tub. Boil as many gallons of water an you have flowers and pour over them. Stir well, cover over with a blanket.

Shere, 1897

COPPER CAULDRON with iron legs in Frensham Parish Church. Probably seventeenth century in date, it has been associated with Mother Ludham the 'witch' who lived in a cave near Moor Park. It is more likely to have belonged to the parish and been used for 'church ales' and other festivities. (*Photographed by Mervin Blatch for this book, by kind permission of the Vicar, the Rev. M.W.H. Kirby*).

Elderberry Wine

TO six gallons of berries with the longer stalks cut off, put 12 gallons of water in a large open pan or tub. Stir up every day with a stout stick for ten days. They will then give off an astrigent smell like tan and the berries will come to the top. This shows they are ready. Boil the whole for about an hour. Take out sme of the liquor and boil in it whole ginger $3/4$ lb., allspice $3/4$ lb. and cloves ½ lb. all bruised. Add it to the bulk when all these have boiled an hour. Then turn it out into the pan on to 30 pounds of Demerara sugar. Stir it up often when cooling to dissolve the sugar. Keep stirring till it has got cooled down to rather warmer than lukewarm. Then put in one pennyworth of Brewer's Yeast floated on "toast to set it " and leave it till next morning. Then take out the toast, leaving most of the yeast, and fill the barrel, leaving some over, about a quart to keep filling up the barrel, as the yeast works out. This will take about six weeks. When it has done working bung it up and keep it in a cool cellar. If well made it improves by keeping a year or two years.

Bramley, 1860

Ginger Beer

FOR 1 Gallon 1 ½ oz of white ginger, 1 lemon cut in slices, 1 lb of lump sugar, a pinch of isinglass, put 4 quarts of boiling water to the above, when nearly cold put 3parts of a table spoonfull of yeast and also of cream of tartar, let it stand all night, skim it, strain it through a piece of calico, bottle it, and in two days it will be fit for use.

Roundhurst, Haslemere, 19th. Century

Orange Wine [and Lemon]

10 Seville oranges, and 1 lemon and 3 lbs of lump sugar, for one gallon of wine. Pare quite half the oranges, and the whole of the lemons, as thin as possible, and put them in a pan or crock, and pour boiling water on them, break the sugar and put it into the barrel, then squeeze the oranges and lemons with your hands until they are quite a pomace* then squeeze the pulp into another pan, and if the water that has been poured on the peel is become quite cold, pour it off on to the pulp and give it another good washing, then squeeze it out again, then put it into a flannel bag, and from the liquor, that the pulp has been squeezed out of both times, on to the sugar, then hang the bag up in a safe place, and continue to pour the water off the peels every morning into the bag of pulp, and the liquor that runs from the bag to be put into the cask until it is full, keeping it stirred every day, when stopped down put in a little Brandy.

Lemon Wine may be made in the same way, excepting it will only require 7 lemons to the gallon to be scalded every day.

Roundhurst, Haslemere, 19th. Century

To make Shrub

ONE quart of Orange Juice, two pounds of Loaf Sugar, two bottles of Rum, two bottles of Brandy, to each quart of Shrub a Large Lemon, mix the whole together in a large Earthenware pan, & stir it on Ten Day or Eight or Nine Days, then put it in a cask, & as soon as fine Bottle it.

Epsom, 19th. Century

Method of making Cyder

LET your apples sweat in heaps some little time to mellow, then pick them and throw away those that are so rotten as to have white specks. Grind them as small as possible so that there be no pecies bigger than a Pea. Let them when ground be together in the pomace about 2 days but no longer before Íou press them; they say the Cyder will be stronger and better coloured.

When you have to barrel up your Cyder, let it be watched carefully when it begins to ferment, and when it begins to get a red Skin, before it has many specks, rack it of. The great nicety is to rack it of before it ferments strong, to prevent it losing its colour and flavour. Tis generally in about 8 days, according to the weather, and about a fortnight after the same again it ferments the second time then rack it for good, and bottle when quite fine in the spring.

N.B. If after the 2nd racking it should ferment a third time rack it again.

Losely MS., Guildford, 17th. to 19th. Centuries. (1379/238)

Mead

TAKE 58½ lbs. Honey - 13 Hops - 13 Lemons. Boil it till no scum arises - which must be taken off - Cut the lemons into boiling liquor & boil ½ hr. and put the peels with the lemons into the cask & add sufficient water to make 13 gallons - Let it stand 9 months, before it is tapped - make between Michaelmas and Christmas.

Grayshott, Hindhead, 1750

* pomace, the mass of crushed apples in the making of Cyder.

The Layout of the Table on March 27th., 1722:

Two quart Pasties at y^r upper end of ye Table
2 fillets stuff of 2 Loins of Veal in 2 dishes
a large H.T. loin of rump of Beef rosted
2 Veal Mutton or Pork Pies, should stand nearby
Any middle or collard flanks of Beef
2 large Cullocks of Beef stuff and boil
2 large Gammons of Bacon boiled
2 small plum puddings baked 2 lbs raisons to each
A Cheshire Cheese cut in two, for there was 2 tables
& this your full quantity will cover them both alike
& is sufficient for 80 - 100 People.

Losely MS., Guildford, 17th. to 19th. Centuries. (1379/1/1)

ACKNOWLEDGEMENTS

I would like to record my grateful thanks to the many private individuals who allowed me to see, record and include their family receipts and "bon mots" and to various institutions, whose staff advised me, displaying much patience with all my requests.

Bourne Hall Museum, Ewell
Farnham Museum, Farnham
Guildford Museum, Guildford
Shere Museum, Shere
Surrey Record Office, Kingston upon Thames
Surrey Record Office, Guildford Muniment Room

Mrs. M. Bedwell
Mrs. G. Clarke
Mrs. G. de Soissons
Mrs. C. Forde
J. Gent, Esq.
K. W. E. Gravett, Esq.
Mrs. M. Hibberd
Miss M. Hide
Mr. & Mrs. D. Hyde

D. C. Marriott, Esq.
Mrs. R. Mason
Mrs. E. Ouston
Mrs. J. Ovington
Mrs. R. Smythe
Miss Y. Weir
Mrs. R. Whitton
Major K. Willis
Mrs. B. Woods

If there is anyone that I have omitted inadvertently, I express my regrets and apologies, and can only hope that they will forgive me.

Daphne Grimm
5th. October, 1991